RESTORED CHRISTIANITY

Donna E. Lane, Ph.D.
& Hayden J. Lane, M.A.

PORTLAND • OREGON
INKWATERPRESS.COM

For Cody

Son and brother, whose amazing spirit is our inspiration,
and whose relationship with Jesus is an example to all.

Table of Contents

Acknowledgements

WE WOULD LIKE TO ACKNOWLEDGE THE IMMEASURABLE CONtributions of Dr. Colin Harris, Dr. Duane Davis, and Dr. Jamie Rasche, in editing, in questioning and clarifying our ideas, and in encouragement. Thanks also to Bonnie Wasson for a beautifully designed cover that illustrates our goal in writing this book; to Erin Rasche for serving as our first editor; to Natalie Menges and Lindsey Lane for acting as our barometers of Christian readers; and, to Dr. David Lane for patience with long hours on the computer and 2 a.m. questions, and for countless contributions of wisdom.

Most of all, thank you, Cody, for your example to us of a fully experienced relationship with Jesus, for the peace and joy with which you live your life, and for your insight and understanding of what it means to live in the moment.

Introduction

THIS BOOK IS A PROJECT OF HOPE, WRITTEN WITH THE GOAL of restoring the Christian church to the foundational beliefs of the teachings and truth of Jesus Christ, based on what we know from the earliest writings following Jesus' resurrection. Our desire is to challenge the children of God to return to a renewed and completely relational knowledge of God. Each chapter will present a different foundational belief, beginning with a description of the current "state" of that subject of belief in today's church. For each issue considered as a part of this book, an historical perspective for both what is known about the initial state of the church regarding that aspect of Christian belief, and how and why developments and changes occurred across the historical continuum will be presented. Then, each chapter will continue with theological implications and a description of the "restored" state of Christianity, concluding with suggestions for what will be required to return to that original condition.

I (Donna) am tasked with presenting the theological portions of our discussion. However, I am not a theologian in the formal or professional sense. I am a Ph.D. Christian counselor, I teach at two universities, and I have been a counselor for almost 30 years, working with a wide variety of populations, issues, and settings. Therefore, I do not bring to this book a theoretical perspective on the theological foundations of Christianity. My point of view has developed through application. I have seen first-hand how certain current beliefs espoused by the church have deeply wounded its members, how those beliefs have reinforced their own false assumptions about life and God and themselves, and where changing those viewpoints to the truth of Christ has brought healing and a closer, healthier relationship with God. I will also pull from my own relationship with Jesus and those truths He has taught me, as they relate to restoring the earliest beliefs of the Christian faith. It is from this stance that I will speak about the importance of and need for the restoration of Christianity.

I (Hayden) will offer the historical perspectives for each chapter. I have a Master's in History, specifically focusing on ancient Greece and Rome, the religions, philosophies, and magical practices of the time, and the beginnings and spread of early Christianity. I have also extensively studied Anthropology, Linguistics, and Classics. These three areas allow me to meld an understanding of ancient history with knowledge about cultures across an historical and geographical continuum, how societies are formed and operate, and how people perceive the world and transmit culture through language.

It is important to understand that I am a different writer with a different perspective, and will present the historical sections as historical analysis. Thus, I will not be making any modern theological claims. Instead, I will be analyzing early Christian belief systems, from the melded perspective of my fields of study, toward presenting a framework and background for the theological sections. Using this perspective, it is my job to examine texts as objectively as possible. While it is impossible for any historian to completely eliminate biases, I will attempt to study early Christian writings from a standpoint of stepping back from any personal beliefs I may hold.

I have had the desire to be a part of a project like this almost as long as I have been studying early Christianity. As I increased in my own knowledge, it became apparent to me that a foundation in historical knowledge is vital for understanding Christianity, both at the time of its conception as well as today. This groundwork is severely lacking in the majority of modern Christians, and is not helped by churches today. The statements I make in my sections are not new information, to historians. However, many of the claims within this book may be new to those who have never felt the need to study the history of the early Christians. I wish to provide small steps toward the creation of this historical foundation, and possibly to spark in you, as a reader, a desire to continue to build upon what I begin.[1]

Together, we will attempt to join history and theology in a unique way, to show that knowledge and faith are not mutually exclusive, and to paint a fully dimensional picture of Who God is and who He says we are. As such, this book does not really "fit" into any category. Typically, scholarly historians reject theological questions and issues of faith from inclusion in their writings as unsubstantiated and impossible to prove, and therefore irrelevant, while writers who expound on faith often ignore scholarly historical research as ungrounded in God's truth, and as such, as potential detractions from faith. Here, we will unite the two disciplines as additive to each other. We believe in the consistency of God, and do not accept that historical fact and theological truth are contradictory. Instead, we stand on the premise that, if both viewpoints are presented accurately, they can "complement" one another. It is our hope that out of that wholeness will grow a deeper, fuller, more grounded and certain, and healthier relationship with God.

However, this type of discussion necessitates an inclusion of warnings for the reader. Certain "sacred cows" of current Christian language and belief are going to be challenged. Nothing is off-limits, from the inerrancy of the Bible to our understanding of the sovereignty of God to the current definition of faith to the meaning of suffering to the contentions of extremely popular Christian authors. At times, issues of faith that you may have been taught your entire Christian walk as absolutes are going to be shaken, and you may feel attacked and defensive. Statements that you may have used to explain life are going to be questioned, and some sense of "security" may be lost. Holes in the present thinking employed by church leaders are going to be exposed. Contradictions caused by flawed logic are going to be revealed. Some things you do not know, and some things you have avoided exploring out of fear that it could alter your faith, are going to be presented and discussed at length. Prepare yourself to be angry...and maybe surprised.

Chapter 1

The Foundations of Restoration

IN OUR PHYSICAL WORLD, A PRINCIPLE CALLED "ENTROPY," PART of the second law of thermodynamics, describes and measures how physical systems tend toward disorder and chaos. The traditional definition of entropy refers to changes in the state or condition of a system, and is a measure of disorder on the molecular level and the amount of wasted energy in any transformation from one state to another.

What, I am sure you are asking, does this superficial discussion of physics have to do with a book on the restoration of Christianity?

During my experiences counseling others, I observed that many basic laws of physics apply to human nature as well. For example, I have identified what I have called "psychological inertia." Inertia in physical sciences is defined as the tendency of an object at rest to stay at rest, or an object in motion to stay in motion, unless acted on by a force. Psychological inertia is the tendency of an individual (or a couple) to stay in their current state unless a strong enough force is exerted on the system to alter the present direction. Another of these physical laws is entropy, the tendency in human nature and psychological systems to move toward chaos. If you don't believe this law of physics applies to humanity like it does to the physical world in which we live, simply put a two year old in your living room and wait for five minutes. What you will find is any and every conceivable object in the room will be transformed into a toy and redistributed chaotically across the floor. Wait an hour and your room will be unrecognizable. Or, if you have a teenager, don't clean his or her room or ask him or her to clean the room for a couple of days. If you can find the floor when you reenter the room, you have a rare teenager indeed! This principle is certainly not restricted to children…I have always secretly wondered why in the world we would "make up" our beds in the morning when we know we are just going to tear them up that evening, and I have often questioned if it is even possible for weekly housecleaning to catch up with the constant influx of belongings, dirt and human destruction. Isn't it a constant complaint of employees that they can never "get ahead," that solving one problem brings on five more? So entropy restated and applied to human nature would go like this: humans and human systems tend toward disorder and chaos, and tremendous energy is wasted in the process of changing from the state of order to disorder.

Christianity and the church corporate, for all of its religious trappings and culture of spirituality, is fundamentally a human system. Thus, the principle of entropy applies to the church as well. If you do not believe the church is primarily a human institution, reflect for a few moments on the actions and role of the church in these topics: the Crusades, the Inquisition, the witch trials, the murder of scientists, the abuses and perversions of the Catholic church prior to the Reformation; or, more recently, bombing abortion clinics, or blaming the sins of the people of New York for 9/11 and saying Hurricane Katrina was God's punishment on New Orleans. Are these the actions of God, or of humans? What about the denominational divisions in the church today? Is denominational division of God, or is Paul's teaching against division and for unity clear enough that the Body of Christ is not to be divided? But it is. Is that God or human entropy?

Just in my lifetime, I have observed a process of entropy occurring in Christianity as a whole, a change that I would describe as tending toward greater chaos, and expending, wasting and losing energy. One evidence of this loss of energy can be seen in the lack of growth, and even the decline, of Christianity as a world religion over the past several years.[2] If such changes have occurred in my relatively short life, what kinds of alterations must have taken place in the fundamental system of Christian beliefs over a period of almost 2000 years?

As indicated in the introduction, the purpose of this book is to examine the transformations in Christianity that have taken place since the death and resurrection of Jesus. We want to attempt to input energy back into the system toward restoring the teachings and truth of Christ to what we know of their original state, or at least to begin the process of moving closer to that original state of being.

Toward this purpose, the current "state" of Christianity will be explored across multiple parameters. An historical perspective will offer a view into what is known about the original state of each current Christian belief identified, and changes across the historical continuum in response to entropy in human nature will be explored. Then, we will present theological implications and a description of the "restored" state of Christianity, built upon the historical foundations, and concluding with suggestions for what will be required to return to that original condition.

Historical Foundations

Any writer who wishes to discuss the historical aspects of the Bible must include a series of caveats, defending his or her case against the immediate defensive position that readers take when their fundamental belief structures are questioned and their sacred texts are reexamined. I would ask that you, as a reader, keep hold of your willingness to listen to new ideas and ways of looking at a book that is actually a series of individual writings that spanned a long period of time and many different regions.

As I have already explained, no modern theological implications will be made in these historical sections. The second half of each chapter will discuss the modern theological aspects. Instead, all I will discuss in the historical perspectives is what is evident by the texts themselves as individual historical documents.

My historical sections will attempt to discuss the theologies of the first Christians. Therefore, the focus of the historical analysis will be on the New Testament, and specifically, the letters of Paul. Paul is the only "first generation" apostle for whom we have words that he himself wrote. While Jesus did not personally teach Paul during his lifetime, I am including Paul among the first generation of apostles for two reasons. First, he authored many letters of what became the New Testament, and his are the earliest writings of Christian belief and theology that we have to examine. Secondly, Paul himself believes that he met Jesus firsthand, and subsequently spent time under the tutelage of the original disciples of Jesus. These were the disciples who lived with Jesus, ate with him, heard his teachings for themselves, and established the first theologies based on direct teaching by Jesus. Aside from a few disagreements with James and Peter, which were eventually resolved, the original disciples accepted Paul's teachings as truth. If they recognized Paul's theology as correct, then Paul must have held beliefs that were not contradictory to their own. Since we do not have anything known to be written by any of the other original apostles, we have, from Paul, a series of letters representing the theology of one of the earliest Christians. This Christian held beliefs that were accepted by the original apostles. He passed on, presumably, the same teachings to all the churches that he established. And his letters represent a record of how the churches altered his teachings and theology, causing him to have to address the problems.

A very important question that now arises is whether or not there was a singular, unified, monolithic "Christianity," which can be uncovered from the historical texts with enough effort. My answer to this question is no. Any monolithic beliefs (if there were any to begin with) of the original "Christians" cannot be viewed as separate from Judaism (which in itself was not monolithic and unified) because the original Christians saw themselves as Jews. By the time Christianity developed its own distinctive identity, there were multiple theologies, "Christianities," if you will.[3] Because of the nature of the church as a social system, it involves groups of people and the cultural context in which they live, thus it was subject to a wide variety of interpretations, due to each individual cultural matrix, and the larger Greco-Roman society in which all early Christians lived. As such, there was dissension among followers of Jesus even from the first generation, as Peter, James, and Paul argued about whether the Gentiles should be included when preaching the gospel. Within the lifetimes of the second generation of Christians, and definitely by the third, human agenda, confusion, and divergent theologies had begun to fundamentally change the directions of the new "Christianities" that emerged.

It is here that I must also digress to explain the "church." Just as there was no monolithic "Christianity," the "Church" was not a unit. Churches were, instead, groups of people in a community or area who met in households together to practice the basic rituals of the religion such as the Eucharist, and to sing and pray. Thus, Paul's use of the word "church" refers only to these groups of people, and not any kind of sacred space or a building in which people gathered for "services." From here on out, when I refer to the church, I am referring to the community of Christians in the area that Paul is addressing his letter (Romans addresses the "church" at Rome).

Returning now to our discussion of Paul's theology, in terms of the Pauline letters included in the New Testament, seven are considered by the majority of historians to be genuinely written by Paul: Romans, I and II Corinthians, Galatians, Philippians, I Thessalonians, and Philemon. Scholarship is divided regarding the authorship of Ephesians, Colossians, and II Thessalonians. I and II Timothy and Titus are generally considered written by another author but ascribed to Paul.[4] Therefore, this analysis will focus only on the "undisputed" letters, those for whom we are certain that Paul was the author, and thus we are certain represent actual Pauline theology.

Many people are unaware that the four Gospels that are part of the New Testament were written years after Paul began preaching. It is a general consensus among historians that none of the Gospels were written by the authors ascribed to them. It is also generally agreed that Matthew, Mark, and Luke, called the "Synoptic Gospels", are based on similar source material and were written earlier than John. Most historians consider John to have been written later and in a different region, due to tain aspects of theology, his sources, and the high Christology of the Gospel with reference to the others. For simplicity's sake, I will continue using the names given to the books and the authors. Most historians, as well as editions of the Bible that contain historical information on the books, believe Mark is the earliest Gospel of the four in the New Testament, written in the sixties. Matthew and Luke, along with Acts, are placed slightly later, in the seventies and eighties. John is thought to have been written somewhere around the turn of the first century.[5]

The synoptic Gospels were not biographies of Jesus in our modern sense. They instead followed the structure of biographies of the time. The Gospels consisted of stories and sayings about Jesus' life that were collected and placed into a narrative structure using connecting words such as "then" and "immediately after" and "at that time." These stories and sayings were meant to illustrate aspects of Jesus' character that the authors wished to present to their audience, more so than factual events. This is very important to the understanding of the Gospels, and more on this and ancient biographies will be addressed in a later chapter.

Many people have in their minds a "conglomerate Gospel," consisting of a melding of various parts of the different stories from each of the four books into their own personal collection of stories and sayings from Jesus, not very dissimilar to the method used by the authors of the four New Testament Gospels. However, just as this individual picture of Jesus is formed as they choose sayings that relate to their own particular situations, struggles, culture, and preferences, when one reads each Gospel independently and with a comparative mindset, differences in the theologies of the authors reveal themselves.

rk places great emphasis on Jesus' miracles, rcisms and healings, and the imminence of Kingdom. Mark includes only a small sec- the text mentioning that Jesus appeared to ...ath, a passage which is considered by many historians to have been added much later by scribes who were disturbed by the Gospel ending with the women fleeing in fear and telling no one about the empty tomb.

In contrast to Mark, Matthew presents Jesus in terms of the Jewish Bible, describing Jesus' family fleeing to Egypt because Herod ordered the killing of all infants under two years, and then returning out of Egypt, where Jesus goes into the wilderness for forty days, emerging to expand on God's law on a mountain, all clear references to the book of Exodus in an attempt to show how Jesus surpassed even Moses. In addition, Herod's infanticide is an atrocious act, which, one would think, should have been mentioned by the two prominent Jewish historians of the time, Josephus and Philo. Both of these historians describe Herod in detail, and most likely would have recorded this event, had the event actually occurred instead of being designed to call Moses to mind.

Luke describes Jesus' birth but has no mention of a trip to Egypt or a slaughter. Instead, the family travels from Nazareth to Bethlehem because of a census by Caesar Augustus who declared that everyone must go back to his or her ancestral hometown. This decree would have uprooted millions of Roman citizens and caused a situation of chaos and disorder which no Roman Emperor would have wanted (would you want such a situation of utter chaos on your hands if you were trying to govern effectively an empire as large as Rome?).

Further analysis shows that while Mark and Matthew are highly apocalyptic texts, Luke has less of an apocalyptic tone, and John greatly diminished the imminence of the end of the world. In addition, John describes Jesus as declaring himself divine with a series of "I am" statements, while Mark has Jesus ordering people not to tell anyone about his miracles or his divine nature.[6] These are but a few examples, meant to serve as a small demonstration of how a comparative analysis of the individual Gospels can illuminate the different theologies of their respective authors. The emergence of these different theological interpretations is due in part to a factor that we might not consider today: the problem of communication due to distance.

As a society that has always had many different forms of mass media and mass communications, automobiles, telephones, and even printed texts, it can be very difficult to imagine how people lived without these means of rapid transportation and communication. Through the Internet, television, radio, and newspapers, pertinent information is sent from the center (i.e. a news studio, printing press, or even a city, state, or national capitol) to the periphery (i.e. you and me). The use of these mediums allows for nearly instantaneous access to all the events happening almost anywhere in the world. Through airplanes and automobiles, newspapers and other printed materials can arrive at their destination on the same day, allowing for slower, yet still daily access to information. Using these means of transportation also allows for a person to travel almost anywhere in the world within one day.

With these miraculous innovations in speed of transportation and communication, it is difficult to imagine how people lived without them. However, an analogous situation can be used to help the process of imagination along. Within almost all of our lifetimes, the Internet did not exist. Think back to how much slower information traveled without this technology. People had to research any topic of interest in a library, taking time out of their day to travel to the building, and then look up the topic in a card catalog, since online databases did not exist, and then find and read the book or article on the subject. There was no e-mail, so any written communication had to be sent through "snail mail," a two-day process at minimum. Even the creation of the term "snail mail" to describe the postal service reflects our experience of how much the Internet has sped up the transmission of ideas. Something that the majority of us have experienced, the dramatic changes in culture and speed of the movement of information that the advent of internet technology has caused, can be related to another dramatic technological innovation: printing.

The technologies we have discussed above: the internet, television, and newspapers, are all dependent on the availability of a way to mass produce printed (or typed, a form of printed) materials which can then be distributed from the center to the periphery in greater supply, allowing for information to be widely spread. The ability to mass-produce literature has the additional effects of increasing the resources available to the commoner; and, as a result, literacy increases. Printing also allows texts to be standardized. Before the printing press, texts were hand copied by scribes, who, because they were human, made unintentional mistakes and sometimes fell victim to the temptation to add something extra to the text.[7] An example of scribal addition can possibly be the ending post-resurrection appearances by Jesus in Mark, as previously discussed. Another example of addenda is the description of Jesus by the Jewish historian Josephus. This description contains, among his historical words about Jesus, attestations that Jesus was the Christ. This declaration seems obviously out of context when compared to the rest of the passage, and when the entirety of his writings show that Josephus was definitely not a Christian (and thus would not profess his faith that Jesus was the Christ).

With the advent of printing, books could be standardized and errors corrected, as shown by the footnotes in your own Bible describing how certain manuscripts include other statements or do not have entire sections of text (While not all Bibles contain this information, the majority do. Check the ending of Mark or the story of the adulteress in John 8). In the time of the first generation of Christians, there was no printing, and information was transmitted mostly orally or by letters. In addition, the majority of the population was illiterate (including, most likely, many of the original apostles), and letters were read out loud.

Taking into account the picture we have all now formed about communication during the first century, it becomes easier to understand how the sheer distance that separated the towns and cities during the first generation of Christians made communication a difficult process. If Paul is an accurate representation of the behaviors of the original apostles, we can surmise that they traveled from place to place, probably by foot, spreading their message in the marketplace or synagogue by word of mouth and founding "churches." After instructing these new churches on the gospel and Jesus' message for a period of time, the apostle would depart to speak other places. This would mean that the new group of believers would be without the instruction of the original teacher for years at a time. This lack of communication led to some serious misinterpretations of the apostles' teachings. Since the only means of communication was by messenger, Paul would send letters, often through one of his disciples (e.g., Timothy, a second-generation follower of Paul) to the different churches, addressing the problems and issues that had arisen. These correspondences form a major part of the New Testament, and people accept them as descriptions of "proper" Christian belief and doctrine. However, the letters illustrate an even greater point: the severity of the changes that occurred in a relatively short time in the doctrines of the first churches.

Even a cursory examination of Paul's letters shows a wide variety of different interpretations of his teachings in the different cities around the Mediterranean. It is a safe assumption that Paul preached a similar message everywhere he visited, so then why was there such a disparate range of problems and misinterpretations among the early churches? Precisely for the reasons stated above. Once Paul left for another city, the members of the church he founded took over leadership, resolving issues as they arose and adding more interpretation to the "gospel" that was passed orally to them through their instruction. Since neither Paul nor the other apostles could be present at every place at all times, they were unable to resolve every problem that arose within the churches. Thus the churches had to take the task on themselves, forming a series of social institutions and instructions, a theology of their own, possibly incorporating aspects of Greco-Roman culture, religion, and philosophy, in order to address issues faced by that region at the time. Even though we do not have any of the letters addressed to Paul from the different churches, it is obvious from his responses that these differences had become very problematic in a short period of time. It stands to reason that these types of alterations and changes continued to occur in Christianity over the intervening centuries, and continue even today.[8]

Where We Go From Here

Well, what do you think so far? Already feeling a bit peeved, a little defensive? What value is there in exploring historical thought about who wrote or didn't write parts of the Bible, when they were written, how early teachings of the gospel were disseminated, and how the Bible was compiled? How does that lead to restoration? This discussion does two things: first, it sets a foundation for you for why we chose the Pauline letters as the *earliest written*, and therefore the closest sources of information to the time of Jesus. Since we are trying to restore Christianity to its earliest "state" we need to know and use the earliest sources of information. Second, it introduces you to the use of historical information for critical thinking and analysis. For example, the fact that many people are unaware the contents of our Bible were not "set" until the 4th century, that there are still books in debate, and that some texts not included in one form of the Bible are used in other forms (Catholic and Greek Orthodox, to name a couple), matters if you are a critical thinker about such things. It affects how we understand the use and purpose of our Bible. It is my belief that closing off our minds when it comes to spiritual matters, while employing critical thinking willingly in other areas of our lives, actually contributes to the isolation and compartmentalization of our relationship with Jesus, holding us back from living fully and experientially our whole lives in the presence of Christ.

Why would we choose to write such an obviously and intentionally controversial book? As I mentioned, I have personally witnessed a transformation in the Church over the past 40 years, and quite frankly, I don't like it. It is not, in my opinion, a change for the better. I am not intimating that the changes have been uniform, but that the tendencies in some areas have not been a positive growth in the direction that Jesus intended. In fact, I see it as movement *away* from what Jesus intended for His children. I observe entropy at work, and I am more and more distressed about where we are as a Body, what we are saying about our Lord, and what we are claiming He said about us. If what I believe is true, that the laws of physics apply to human nature and human systems, then the only thing that can alter the course of this entropy is an input of new energy. This must not be just a simple amount of energy; it must be energy great enough to undo the work of entropy, greater than the energy expended (and wasted) in the transformation to our current condition.

When I read Old Testament prophets, or the recorded words of John the Baptist, or the writings of the apostle Paul, I do not read words spoken hesitantly, couched in concern for what people thought or how the words made people feel, or cushioned out of fear. I see instead words spoken boldly, as Paul described, fearlessly taking a stand. I see them opposing human entropy, and challenging people to redirect their lives toward God. Now I do not compare myself in any way to these great people, but I use them as the example I am supposed to follow.

Having been forewarned, we ask only that you approach each chapter with a mind and heart open to the leadings of the Holy Spirit. We promise to do the same.

Chapter 2

The Bible and the Holy Spirit

The Current State of the Church and the Bible

THE HISTORICAL DISCUSSION IN THE PREVIOUS CHAPTER ON the changes brought about by the advent of the printing press makes clear why, as soon as the capability was present, human beings desired to have the teachings of God in transmissible, written form, that would not be altered by individual scribes or human error. Jewish scribes had been writing and rewriting the Torah for centuries, so there was a precedent in Judaism for sacred writings, something that did not necessarily exist in other religions at the time of the development of the early Christian church. However, I believe we sometimes forget that the first Christians; indeed, Christians up through the 4th century, had no standardized set of sacred writings at all, beyond the Torah (or for most, who could not read Hebrew, the Greek Septuagint). It is almost as though we imagine Paul and Timothy showing up at a house church, pulling out their Bibles and preaching based on some chapter and verse they chose from the sacred text, using those sacred writings as their authority.

Of course, the image of Paul carrying a pocket Bible with him around the Mediterranean is quite false. However, this picture seems to be almost assumed by the church. For example, I was at a church-sponsored event, and the speaker quoted from Colossians 3:16, "Let the word of Christ dwell in you richly." He then went on to say, "What Paul meant by this is that we are supposed to read and study the Bible every day." A picture of Paul handing out pocket New Testaments in the King James Version to all the Christians in Colosse as part of his ministry came to my mind. Is that really what Paul (if indeed those words were written by Paul) meant? If so, he was instructing the people of Colosse to read and study a book that would not exist for over 200 years, which seems silly and pointless. If not, what did Paul mean by "the word of Christ"? We will explore that very question in this chapter.

Perhaps having a set of identified sacred texts to follow created a sense of security for the Christians who first had those texts available to them, and it seems that sense of reliance has grown across the years.

Based on our current view and reliance on the Bible, I have wondered how those first Christians knew what to believe without a Bible to guide them? How did they proceed without the "inerrant, infallible, authoritative Word of God"? How could they presume to preach "the Word" if they had no "Word" to use?

To find an answer, I simply need to look in the sacred writings available to those first Christians, Jeremiah 31:33-34:

'This is the covenant I will make with the house of Israel after that time,' declares the Lord. 'I will put my law in their minds and write it on their hearts. I will be their

God, and they will be my people. No longer will a man teach his neighbor, or a man his brother, saying, 'Know the Lord,' because they will all know me, from the least of them to the greatest,' declares the Lord.

These verses seem to be saying that, under the new covenant (following the coming of Messiah); we will no longer need to teach each other about Who our Lord is, because we will all *know* Who He is, personally, and specifically, in our hearts.

Reading those verses, would you say they describe the current state of the Church? Is the truth of God written on our hearts? Do we as Christians look at each other, from the least to the greatest, and say we all know the Lord?

Because the answer to that question is "no," at least in my experience, I believe we have become more and more reliant on the Bible, our "sacred texts," to teach us how to know the Lord, and to instruct us as to Who the Lord is. Let me use this example to present this point more clearly. Let's say that someone who knows me, even someone who knows me very well - my best friend, for example - goes to a church where no one has ever met me. She sets out then to describe me to the people in that church. She tells them how I am a tall woman, she gives them details on my personal beliefs as she understands them, she describes my hair style and color, the kind of clothes I wear, my clunky shoes and my enjoyment of a good, intelligent discussion, and she describes in her own language my vehemence when someone disparages my Lord. The people in that church are interested, and they pay close attention. When she is finished, they can say they know all about me. If someone else asks them, they can also describe me as tall, with longish hair and interesting clothes, someone who doesn't mind defending the Lord against those who speak falsely about Him. (OK, so they left out the part about liking intelligent discussion, and they used different words, but you would still get the gist, right?) Can those people say they know me? If, two weeks later, I walked into that church, would everyone automatically declare, "that is Donna!"? Could, if asked, any of them give a correct, precise answer to my opinion on birth control or global warming? Most importantly, could any one of them honestly say they knew how it *felt* to be with me? No, because they might know *about* me, but they do not *know* me.

Similarly, I believe that because of our reliance on the Bible, identified by Church Leaders (not by Jesus for obvious reasons, since it didn't exist and since He, at least according to the book of John, taught His disciples that He is the Word made flesh) as the "infallible, inerrant Word of God," we as a Body have generally come to the place where we know about God, but we do not know Him personally, nor is His truth written on our hearts. We can, using the Bible as our authority, talk about Who He is, but if He walked in the room today, would we recognize Him? Is this current condition the very reason, in fact, that we as a Body are so defensive about the inerrancy of Scripture, because we revere it as our only source of knowing about God?

So, to describe our current state in reference to the Bible, I would say we worship the Bible, and use the Holy Spirit as a tool. And I would say this position is exactly backwards.

Now let's examine how we arrived where we are.

Historical Analysis

Paul begins his letter to the church at Galatia with a curse: "But even if we or an angel from Heaven should preach a gospel other than the one we preached to you, let him be eternally condemned (Galatians 1:8)." As we have already seen through a very small series of examples, the four "authoritative" descriptions of Jesus' life, the Gospels of the New Testament, were written after Paul's ministry and differ greatly among themselves in describing Jesus' message, ideas about himself, and theology. If Paul himself warns the early church not to trust another gospel besides the one he preached, how can Christians today accept four clearly differently motivated and even sometimes contradictory stories, with different descriptions of the protagonist, as completely inerrant?

It must then be our effort to discover what the message of Paul's gospel was.

People today associate "gospel" with biography, and the four "Gospels" are biographies of Jesus' life. However, this is not what Paul seems to mean when he describes preaching the "gospel," because he includes very little in the way of quotations from Jesus or stories of his life. Within the seven undisputed Pauline letters, there are only a handful of statements describing events of Jesus' life, his teaching, or his character before his crucifixion, as recorded by the four Gospel traditions. Of these examples from Paul's letters, he quotes examples of Jesus' teaching only three times, specifically claiming that the "Lord" said what he wrote. Additionally, these three quotations all occur in the same letter: I Corinthians 11:24-26 presents a form of the events of the Last Supper and contains the quotations from Jesus about the body and blood, and I Corinthians 7:10 and I Corinthians 9:14 echo Jesus' teaching on divorce and receiving money for ministry respectively. Outside of direct references to Jesus' teachings, the remainder of Paul's descriptions is about Jesus' life and character. II Corinthians 10:1 and Philippians 2:7-8 describe Jesus' character as meek and gentle, humble and obedient with the nature of a servant. Romans 1:3 states that Jesus was a descendant of David, and Galatians 4:4 states that Jesus was born of a woman and under Jewish law. Finally,

Galatians 4:6 and Romans 8:15 contain the same explanation that because of Jesus, we cry *"abba, father."* This is possibly a reference to Jesus' addressing God as *abba*, Aramaic for father, in his prayers, as also recorded by Mark (however, Paul does not state that the words are from the Lord, as he does with other quotations).[9]

Digressions aside, this is a noticeable lack of inclusion of events which would seem very relevant, even vital, especially after reading the four Gospels that start the New Testament. Instead, Paul's own description of the gospel that he preached is very straightforward:

> Now, brothers, I want to remind you of *the gospel I preached to you,* which you received and on which you have taken your stand. *By this gospel you are saved,* if you hold firmly to the word I preached to you. Otherwise, you have believed in vain. For what I received I passed on to you as of first importance (Alternate translation: I passed on to you at the first): that Christ died for our sins according to the Scriptures (i.e. according to exegesis from the prophecies of the Jewish sacred texts), that he was buried, that he was raised on the third day according to the Scriptures, and that he appeared to Peter, and then to the Twelve. After that, he appeared to more than five hundred of the brothers at the same time... Then he appeared to James, then to all the apostles, and last of all he appeared to me also, as to one abnormally born (I Corinthians 15:1-8, NIV, italics added for emphasis).

This is an example of one of the earliest Christian creeds, which Paul "received" by "revelation from Jesus Christ" (Galatians 1:11-12) and from the original disciples, and then taught to all of the churches he founded. This declaration may have been recited by the members of the earliest churches. People have read this creed *ad infinitum* in church, Bible studies, and in their own studies. But, just as with the prior analysis of the Gospels, if it is examined with a different perspective, this creed reveals what was of most importance to Paul, and by extension the other apostles. A major point of significance in the creed, which Paul states is the "gospel," is that nothing of Jesus' pre-crucifixion life or ministry is mentioned. There is no birth story, no baptism, no temptation in the desert, no healings, no Sermon on the Mount, no walking on water, no exorcisms, no adulterous woman, no transfiguration, no raising of Lazarus, no conversation with Pilate, no casting of lots for his clothes, no Passion of the Christ. The Gospel begins when Christ "died." The only events recorded are his post-resurrection appearances.

Now I am not arguing here that none of the events recorded about Jesus in the four Gospel traditions happened, only that they are not existent in this creed. There are three possible ways to explain this exclusion of Jesus' life from Paul's gospel: one; that Paul did include stories and examples from Jesus life, but because of his writing style, did not openly quote Jesus, two; that he knew nothing of the events, or three; that he did not see the events as important. However, Paul extensively quotes the Jewish Bible for support of his arguments, evidence that he does in fact employ outside references in his writing style, and does (albeit rarely) directly quote Jesus. If stories and words of teaching from Jesus himself were circulating, would Paul not have wanted to support his contentions with words directly from Jesus, as he does on the three occasions in I Corinthians? Additionally, if we accept that Paul spent time with and received instruction from the original disciples, who were active parts of

Jesus' ministry, it is highly unlikely that Paul did not know of the events that transpired during Jesus' life. Thus we are left with the final option, that it was unimportant. If it was unimportant to know about Jesus' life and teaching, then what was important?

If, as Paul himself declares, the statement he made to the Corinthians was the contents of the gospel that he received and then passed on to the church, then the "gospel" of Jesus Christ for the original Christians was that Jesus died, was raised, and appeared to various people as proof of his resurrection. This is a fairly simple message, and one not very informative about how to deal with problems arising from daily life. As we have discussed earlier, after founding churches, the first-generation founder would be absent for long periods of time, leaving the new church to have to solve problems for themselves. If stories about Jesus' life were already circulating from church to church by word of mouth, it is fairly easy to imagine one attributing a piece of philosophy or an event to Jesus simply to give authority to a method of dealing with a situation.

The attribution of words and deeds to people is not uncommon in the ancient world, nor was it seen as spreading falsehoods. We have already discussed how the writers of the canonical Gospels collected circulating stories about Jesus to illustrate points about his character. This was one of the methods of biography for the Greco-Roman world. Actual words and deeds were less important than providing examples that illustrate good or bad qualities of a person. For instance, in the late first century the writer Plutarch authored a work entitled *Parallel Lives*, in which he compares the lives of notable Greeks, paralleled with the lives of notable Romans. For example, one set of parallel lives compares Alexander the Great with Julius Caesar. Alexander and Caesar did not experience the same historical events throughout their lives, but Plutarch pairs them because they serve, for him, as examples of the same aspects of character. These stories are read side by side in order to represent the similarities of their characters, and the reporting of actual historical events is more or less irrelevant, because that was not the goal of the work. This is a single example, but serves to illustrate the point that Greco-Roman biographies were often not viewed the same way we perceive a biography today.

Thus, early Christians used this accepted biographical method to illustrate Jesus' character, or to provide authority to a statement. Again, this is not an accusation about the integrity of the early Christians; it was simply a different method of looking at the world.[10] To create an analogous situation, we have no words from Jesus about how to deal with speed limits, or handguns, or internet pornography, yet this does not prevent people from taking what they think they know about Jesus' character and applying that to issues that were not in existence at the time. The question of "What would Jesus do?" is posed, and based on examples of his character, people can claim that Jesus would say "Thou shalt not speed." Is this spreading falsehood? Most people would say not.

When examining these issues, however, it is no wonder that Paul had to write to Galatia about people "trying to pervert the gospel of Christ." Stories about Jesus' life circulated widely, becoming more and more sensational. As problems needed solving throughout the churches, events from Jesus' life, real or created, became reflections of or solutions to these crises. For example, "The Jews," a nameless mob who are prevalent in John as the antagonists to Jesus, are a clear reflection of later social problems regarding the relations between Jews and Christians. Since Jesus and the earliest followers of his teachings were

Jewish, the separation of Jesus and the disciples from "the Jews" reflects a later situation in which Christians had developed a self identity apart from Judaism and were experiencing social strife with the Jewish population. In contrast to this description, Mark portrays Jesus receiving conflict from the scribes and Pharisees, those who interpret Jewish Law. That Jesus would debate legal aspects with experts in the law still reflects his close connection with Judaism. Thus Mark, an earlier text, reflects Christianity's close association with Judaism, whereas in John the division has already been clearly made, such that Jews become a separate and outside enemy.[11]

In addition, people have a need to fill in gaps in the story of the life of their religious hero. As we have already discussed, there were at least two separate birth traditions circulating, collected by Matthew and Luke. There were probably more, though we do not have examples of them. Authors took it upon themselves to provide examples of Jesus as a child, and, as we have already discussed, to insert aspects of their own theology into the stories. The Infancy Gospel of Thomas tells stories of Jesus as a child, leading up to the incident described in Luke where the boy Jesus stayed behind at the Temple. In this gospel, young Jesus begins as a precocious supernatural kid with a bit of a mischievous side. We meet the boy Jesus sculpting pigeons out of clay, and when he is chastised for working on the Sabbath, he brings them to life. In another example, Jesus and a peer are playing on a rooftop, when the child falls and dies. The village blames Jesus for pushing the child, but Jesus brings him back to life to prove his innocence. Jesus has several run-ins with teachers as well, always outsmarting them. These stories, while entertaining, were written to illustrate a theological point about Jesus' life: that he was endowed with divine power from his birth, and not at his baptism as the theologies of some groups at the time claimed. Thus we have an example of a collection of stories about Jesus meant to fill gaps in the narrative of Jesus' life and illustrate a theological point.

There were, of course, other "Christianities" that emerged through the second and third centuries, as varied in their theologies as the different denominations are today. Gnosticism, a sect that has recently gained renewed interest due to the rediscovery of the "Gospel of Judas," told its own set of stories about Jesus to reinforce its set of theologies and institutions, just as the other Christianities had done. While Gnostics were no more monolithic than any other branch of the milieu of early "Christianities," on the whole they believed that salvation came through secret *gnosis*, knowledge and understanding that God provides only to those able to receive it. Aspects of the varied theologies among the Gnostics included the idea that Jesus was a human man upon whom the Spirit descended at his baptism and left him at the crucifixion, prompting Jesus' cry, "My God, my God, why have you forsaken me?" Marcionism, another Christian theology that developed in the mid second century, argued that Jesus came to overthrow the evil creator God of the Old Testament. These two examples are a small illustration of how, by the third century, there were multiple Christianities with numerous stories circulating about Jesus, all regionally spread and reinforced, and all relating to different aspects of his character in terms of the culture and theology that each church or region developed and adopted. But there was no universally recognized set of orthodox canonized texts through the first three centuries of the development of Christianity.

Canonization of the New Testament spanned a long period of time and was not truly resolved until after the Protestant Reformation. A brief overview of this process begins with Marcion, the founder Marcionism. When discussing the "Bible" in the middle of the second century, he counted only a version of Luke and some of the Pauline letters as authentic. The rest, including the entire Old Testament, he dismissed. The Bishop Irenaeus counted the four Gospels as authentic when writing around 180. Eusebius, who was present at the first Council of Nicea in 325, where an attempt was made to standardize the ritual dogma and sacred texts of the "one holy catholic and apostolic Church," presented a list of New Testament texts in his *Ecclesiastical History* as the four Gospels, Acts, the letters of Paul, the epistle of John, the epistle of Peter, and Revelation. The first example of the set of books which we recognize as canon today was given by Athanasius, the Bishop of Alexandria, in 367. This canon was finally approved at the third council of Carthage in 397. Even after this agreement, canon of certain books was still disputed, especially James and Revelation. Martin Luther questioned, but ultimately did not dismiss, the authenticity of James, Jude, Hebrews, and Revelation even in the sixteenth century.[12] Debates about the authenticity of Scripture happening all the way up to the sixteenth century illustrate clearly that the Bible took much time and many evolutions to develop into the form we revere today.

Restored View of the Bible

Having now heard the arguments historically against an inerrant and infallible text, I would like to turn the discussion in a different direction. As a starting point, I want to propose these questions:

1) Why does the Bible exist and what is its usefulness to us?
2) If we accepted the errancy and fallibility of the current text, what would that do to our beliefs?
3) Why do we feel we *need* the Bible to be inerrant and infallible?

Do we have a set of sacred texts for a reason? Yes, I believe the Bible is useful to us and exists for a purpose. Paul expresses his belief that his written words are truth taught to him by the Spirit (I Corinthians 2:13) and confirmed in his conscience by the Spirit (Romans 9:1). Paul also states that the gospel he preached was revelation from Jesus Christ (Galatians 1:11-12). However, Paul is clear that he dictated his letters (Romans 16:22) and wrote at least some parts by his own hand (I Corinthians 16:21, Philemon 1:19). He gives no indication at any point that the texts of his letters appeared before him magically, or that the writing implement produced the words on the page separate from his direction. Therefore, I believe, as Paul indicates, that he wrote his letters to convey the gospel's truth, as inspired by the Holy Spirit. Do I think God took up a pen and wrote Paul's letters? No I don't. Paul wrote his letters, as letters, in response to specific questions asked him by newly formed churches, not as a book for people to idolize and worship in the Holy Spirit's stead. However, I do believe the Holy Spirit guided Paul into truth as Paul wrote his letters. I believe God partners with us in such things by His choice and desire. I believe the Holy Spirit is given to guide *all* His children into His truth, and the Bible is a tool we can use, as the basic truths of God written down by men who knew Jesus, or knew those who knew Jesus, and who had received His Holy Spirit. I believe, therefore, that the Bible is inspired, and by that I mean Holy Spirit partnered.

I also believe that the Bible is authoritative, and what I mean by that statement is that it speaks with authority on the truth of God. 'Now wait,' you may be saying, 'I thought you just argued that it was not infallible or inerrant? How can you then state that it contains the truth?' I believe there is a difference between the truth and historical facts. To me, it is similar to asking the question is the Bible literal? Of course not. The visions of the Old Testament prophets, the dream interpretations of Daniel, and Messiah portrayed as a Lamb and His people as sheep are just a few examples of intentional symbolism designed to represent a greater lesson or point. Jesus told parables (stories designed to teach specific lessons), and he did not intend by those stories for us to literally go purchase a field, spend our lives searching for a pearl, throw seeds along a path, live in a pen like sheep, plant a mustard seed to watch it become a tree, or try to make Pike's Peak move to Wyoming.

Does the Bible, however, convey the character of Christ to us, and does it present the "gospel" as described by Paul (Recall what we identified earlier in this chapter as "the gospel" according to Paul's writings)? Yes, it does, clearly. As Christ *is* the truth, and the Bible conveys, from the beginning of the Old Testament through to the end of the New Testament, the character of Christ, the Bible communicates the truth.

Consider these questions for a moment: what if God did not intend for us to rely on a written text for our knowledge of Him? What if, as suggested in 2 Timothy 3:16, the texts of the Jewish Scriptures were "useful for teaching, rebuking, *correcting* and training in righteousness, so that the *man of God* may be thoroughly equipped for *every good work* (italics added for emphasis)."? What if God intended His children to *know* Him rather than know *about* Him? What if the written texts were to be used by the people of God as a tool, in preparation for good works and training in righteous behavior, instead of worshipped as a perfect replacement for God's Presence? This idea was present at the writing of Paul's letters, the earliest writings we have on Jesus' gospel, which describe the role of the Holy Spirit in knowing God in this way:

The Spirit searches all things, even the deep things of God. For who among men knows the thoughts of a man except the man's spirit within him? In the same way no one knows the thoughts of God except the Spirit of God. We have not received the spirit of the world but the Spirit who is from God, that we may understand what God has freely given us. This is what we speak, not in words taught us by human wisdom but in words taught by the Spirit, expressing spiritual truths in spiritual words. The man without the Spirit does not accept the things that come from the Spirit of God, for they are foolishness to him, and he cannot understand them, because they are spiritually discerned. The spiritual man makes judgments about all things, but he himself is not subject to any man's judgment: 'For who has known the mind of the Lord that he may instruct him?' But we have the mind of Christ. (I Corinthians 2:10-16).

The idea was also present at the writing of the canonical Gospel texts, as indicated by the inclusion of Jesus informing His disciples, "And I will ask the Father, and he will give you another Counselor to be with you forever - the Spirit of truth. The world cannot accept him because it neither sees him nor knows him. But *you know him*, for he lives with you and *will be in you* (John 14:16-17, italics added for emphasis)." So, it is through the presence of the Holy Spirit within us that we know God and God's truth.

The Bible can then be used as a tool with which we can compare the truth presented through the Holy Spirit's presence of Jesus' character against what we know of His character in Scripture, not to test God but to test our discernment, for truth will always match truth (even if presented fact does not always match presented fact).

Go back for just a moment to my example of my friend describing me to her church. Having described me in some detail, let's pretend she brings another friend to church with her the following Sunday, and introduces her as Donna. However, this other friend is of slight build, and does not speak up about her faith or speak out when someone presents something in Sunday school about God contrary to His character. The inconsistencies would lead the church members to question my friend if this person was really the Donna she described to them previously. At that questioning, she could then inform them, "No, this is not Donna LANE, this is Donna SMITH," and clear up the misunderstanding. But if I came to the church and my friend introduced me as Donna, and they could see that I was indeed tall, and in Sunday school I immediately started speaking up about my beliefs, generating discussion and confronting false statements about the character of God, the class would not hesitate to receive me as the Donna described by my friend. It is in this way that the Bible can be a valuable and necessary *tool* for our use. It simply cannot *replace* meeting and knowing God personally for ourselves.

Which brings me to the second question: what does this do to our beliefs? I have heard people speak, both nonbelievers and believers, as if the fallibility of the Bible precludes their ever accepting God or continuing to believe in Him. This total dependency on a book instead of on God is precisely one of the problems I have with where the church is today, in relation to the Bible. The debate over the inclusion or exclusion of the story in John of the adulteress saved from stoning by Jesus' response to her accusers does not undermine or confirm my belief in Jesus. I believe in Jesus because I have met Him! The fact that this story is not present in the earliest manuscripts is irrelevant to me. It is a *good story*! More to the point, it illus trates the character of Christ extremely well, and is consistent with the character of Christ as portrayed throughout the entire Bible. Based on my knowing Him, would Jesus as I know Him have said and done something like that? Certainly. Is this story, then, "truth"? I would say yes, absolutely. Is it "fact"? I would respond, "Irrelevant."

Someone might ask, "Then how do we know Jesus was crucified and resurrected, if facts are open for debate?" Ah, but now you are back to the original "gospel" as taught by Paul and the first apostles. This fact, as you recall, was all that Paul resolved to know when preaching in Corinth (I Corinthians 2:2), and what Paul taught "as of first importance" (I Corinthians 15:3-4). This *is* the "gospel."

It is my contention, then, that it would benefit rather than destroy or undermine our belief to recognize and accept the errors and flaws in the collection of writings we call the Bible. If I do so, I don't have to resort to denial or preposterous claims to make myself feel secure (such as the claim that the earth is really only 6000 years old, give or take a few years, and dinosaurs were on the Ark with Noah…in case you are not aware, the fossil record indicates dinosaurs were extinct for millions of years before the appearance of man). If the Bible was never intended to be a factual history of man, I don't have to alter historical facts to make them match the Bible or accuse scientists of being antichrists simply because they discover a new scientific fact that makes me uncomfortable with my Bible. My security can then remain where it belongs: in Jesus and Jesus alone. I can resolve, as Paul, to know only Christ and Him crucified.

In addition, I would be forced to rely on the presence of the Holy Spirit within me to know God, to know God's thoughts and will, and to receive His truth while actually feeling His love.

31

The unintended positive consequences of this shifting reliance from the Bible to the Holy Spirit for truth would be appropriate humility in the face of my inability to know truth without the Spirit of God, and a lessening of self-reliance on my mental ability to figure it all out, something that would also be consistent with the nature and character of Christ. According to Paul, "The mind of sinful man is death, but the mind controlled by the Spirit is life and peace (Romans 8:6)." Paul goes on the say that "those who are led by the Spirit of God are sons of God (Romans 8:14)," but "if anyone does not have the Spirit of Christ, he does not belong to Christ (Romans 8:9)."

So we come to the last question: why is it that we have come to rely so heavily on the Bible, such that we feel a deep need for the Bible to be inerrant and infallible? I would answer this question, as so many others in this book, with what we have lost from what was known from the first. I am aware that many, or even most, pastors talk about the Holy Spirit (or Jesus) living in our hearts. Many talk about accepting Christ into our hearts to be saved. Take a few moments, though, and explore your memories to see when was the last time your pastor talked about the "what's" and "how's" of Jesus' Spirit living within us. How often does your pastor teach on how to listen to God, to see Him, to have a heart-to-heart conversation with God, to feel His Presence within your heart, to feel His arms around you comforting you in times of pain and sorrow? How often have you heard your pastor describing his or her own experiences of seeing His face, hearing His voice, feeling His touch?

My experience has been that the context of these sermons, if they occur at all, focuses on spiritual disciplines. Focusing on spiritual disciplines brings the belief right back to self-reliance and leaves the listener with a sense of needing to "do it right" or "get it right" in order to elicit a response from God. And most often the first discipline mentioned is Bible study, followed by the statement, "if you want to hear from God, read His Word." We are prescribed daily, structured reading, often with a commentary or devotional to tell us what the Bible is saying. No one stops to think how this process pulls us two steps away from hearing directly from God. Then, of course, when we fail (for we will) to meet the obligation of daily hours of study for "should's" sake, we begin a process of horrible self-condemnation. Instead of the loving heart of God, we feel a sense of worthlessness, as if we could never be good enough to know God...and we are now three steps away from what we truly need.

Another popular spiritual discipline mentioned is prayer. For me, the word "prayer" has become so tainted by human misuse that I almost want to come up with a new word to describe an ongoing conversation with God. "Pray without ceasing" (I Thessalonians 5:17) is perverted into an instruction to set aside a time for daily prayer where we follow a structured format, where we go through the six or twelve or however many steps (I call this a "list of six") described for "effective prayer" and become the Stepford Wives on autopilot. May I point out, however, that Paul was rather notorious for saying exactly what he meant? Therefore, praying without ceasing means praying without ceasing: an ongoing, never ending, never stopping, every waking second conversation with God in our hearts, during which we share every experience, from a morning cup of coffee to mourning the loss of a loved one.

I am suggesting that this precious experience has been, for the most part, lost to us as a Body. I cannot tell you how many people in Sunday school classes, in my counseling office, or in my university classes, having heard me talk about my experiences with Jesus, have asked me to tell them *how*. I can see it in their eyes, and hear it in their tone of voice. They are starving to know God; they want to see Him and hear Him and to touch and be touched by Him...but they don't know where to begin, and another "list of six" is just not going to cut it. And, somehow, they *know* that.

Beginning in this chapter, and continuing throughout the remainder of the book, we will attempt to put together answers to those pressing questions of "what" and "how." A problem faced in trying to describe this type of relationship with Jesus in a book is that it can be taken as another list of "to do's," or a set of prescribed steps to follow, a "list of six." Neither of those outcomes is our intention. First, each individual relationship with Jesus is unique, just like each friendship or marriage is unique based on the distinctive qualities of the individuals that make up the relationship. To dictate a universal list of steps to follow is to remove or deny that individuality. Could I write a book that tells you exactly what your particular spouse wants from you in a relationship? No, I could not, not without knowing you both personally, no matter how skilled or experienced I am with marriage issues. However, there are commonalities in marriage that I could address, pitfalls I could prepare you to avoid, and healthy attitudes I could describe and encourage that generally make for marital success.

Second, all relationships exist in states of being rather than doing, and what we do in the relationship flows out of who we are with each other. An intimate relationship with Jesus is no exception, and to establish a list of "to do's" is to thwart the reality of the relationship as a "be." I can, however, talk about "being" with Jesus as I have experienced it, and I can offer you options and choices from which to begin to establish your own individual and unique ways of being with Him. I can reveal those hindrances that consistently interfere with an intimate relationship with Jesus. For example, certain beliefs about God have been taught as "truth," when they have actually arisen as an explanation or self-justification for why we are not experiencing the intimacy and "realness" we desire with God. As a result, the Body of Christ in general does not expect to have that type of relationship with God. And, not seeking it, we, of course, do not find it.

Finally, a "list of six" and a set of "to do's" both set the reader up to fail, to feel inadequate to a task, to believe in a "can't," to feel shame and condemnation, and to experience isolation as if there is something fundamentally wrong with them that they didn't "do it right." All of these beliefs are false. We request, therefore, that to the best of your ability you take responsibility for not interpreting anything that follows as a list of steps or a set of prescribed "to do's," remembering the warnings issued and limitations described here and knowing that we did not intend what we say in that way. We also request that you read each new chapter as additive, but not systematic. Meaning, don't interpret what we are saying in each chapter as "the next step" in a process as if there is an order or system to follow, but instead read each chapter as adding to a whole picture of an experience.

As the premise of this book is a restoration of Christianity to its original (earliest known) state, we will want to examine how this process took place for the first Christians. How, for example, did Paul describe an intimate relationship with the Lord to those he taught "the gospel"? We will address these kinds of questions further in later chapters. In the context of this chapter's topic, we can clearly say that Paul did not suggest that his new believers read the Bible in order to know God: first, it did not exist, and second, Paul was relying on the Holy

Spirit to accomplish that goal. To us, this makes perfect sense, because you cannot have a relationship with a book.

Consequently, if you decide to ditch the idea of Bible reading as the way to know God, and you choose to adopt the Bible as a useful tool instead, may I suggest that you change your expectations of God as well? I believe that we look for what we expect. For example, if I am walking through the forest and I expect to see beauty there, I will be looking at the wonderful way the sunlight flickers down through the leaves and glistens off the droplets of water. I will notice the rich colors and shapes of the different plants, and I will be seeking a glimpse of some lovely forest animal like a deer hiding among the trees or sipping from a brook. If, however, I expect to see fearful things in the forest, I will be checking under rocks and on tree limbs for bugs and snakes, and that is exactly what I will find! So, if we change our expectations of God, I believe we will seek God according to those altered expectations. If I do not expect God to be present unless I am kneeling in a prayer closet, sitting in church, or reading my Bible, then I will not perceive Him in all the other times. If, however, I expect Him to be "ever-present," based on the truth that "nothing can separate me from the love of God in Christ Jesus," then I will look for Him, the same way I will look for and notice the beauty I expect to find in the forest.

I expect God to always be with me, present and real and responsive. He is my very best friend in the whole wide world, and He has nothing else He would rather be doing. In fact, He *prefers* to be with me; He *wants* to be with me and to share all of my life experiences. These are truths I know in my heart. When I wake up in the morning, He is there to greet me. When I get in my car to drive to work, He sits with me and keeps me company. When I walk into a counseling session, He is my partner and at times my supervisor. When I am preparing for a class, He offers suggestions. When I am teaching the class, He prompts my thoughts. In those moments of sadness or distress over my son's illness, He comforts me and encourages me. From the mundane to the intense, from the everyday to the exceptional, He is the first Presence. He is my partner in all things. This constancy and this partnership are what I expect from Him…and it is what I find. These are my experiences.

Chapter 3

The Old Testament and New Testament View of God

The Current State of the Church and How We See God

JUST AS OUR VIEW AND USE OF THE BIBLE HAS BEEN DISTORTED through the years due to a loss of the intended intimate connection with God, our view of God has been distorted by distance and our own perceptions imposed on Him. This includes Who we believe He is, what we think we can expect from Him, and how we relate to Him. One critical issue that has changed is our current belief in a division within God's nature. It is as if we see Him as two different "gods," the God of the Old Testament and the God of the New Testament.

The "Old Testament God" has become to us the God of wrath and anger, like the Punisher on steroids or a police officer with a bad attitude and a lot of power, passing out his vigilante justice and sending down lightning bolts to keep us in line. In contrast, we have transformed the "New Testament God" into our Santa Claus, bestowing gifts as long as we are good enough to earn them, magically raining down money and trinkets that we call "blessings," but only if we do the right things, pray the right prayers, and "give Him the glory." Our current view makes Him seem like a narcissistic bipolar co-dependent. On the one hand, our "God" is arrogant, prideful, and capricious; and we had better get it right! On the other hand, we see ourselves as able to control and manipulate His responses simply based on what we do, almost as if we believe He has no "will" of His own but only reacts to us. He is a blaming, shaming, hateful wretch - Who "loves us so much." Of course, both of these perceptions cannot be true, and having such disparate beliefs in our minds causes what is called "cognitive dissonance." So we keep the "two gods" separate, and pull out the one that we feel is called for or the one we think we can best "use," depending on our circumstances.

The story of Job comes to mind here. This story gives us two examples of what I am describing. First, we see the attitude of God as Santa Claus in Satan's challenge to God, where the father of lies suggests that Job loves and honors God only because of all the "things" he has been given. Then we hear Job's friends describing God as the punishing police officer, insisting to Job that he must have sinned greatly for God to penalize him so severely that he lost all of his "blessings" and is now suffering. Yet, these descriptions from the mouths of Satan and Job's friends are not very different from what we hear today.

I am left to wonder who in their right minds would ever completely trust this divided God? Who would willingly choose to put their whole lives into the hands of someone like He is described today? And what kind of intimate relationship can we ever hope to have with such a "God"?

Historical Analysis

Our goal is to try to recapture the beliefs of the first generation of Christians, through Paul. Paul's letters and his beliefs will be employed and analyzed in order to explain how the earliest followers of Christ perceived the character of God. We have already explored the historical origins of a division between the God of the Old Testament and the God of the New. As we previously examined, the idea of two gods from the Old and New Testaments is not a new one. If you recall, in the second century, Marcionism surfaced as one of the myriad of Christian theologies. It taught that Jesus was the good God of the New Testament who came to overthrow the evil Creator "demiurge" of the Old Testament. However, the question remains, what were the earliest Christians' views on the Old Testament God and Jesus? Again, as this is the historical analysis, no modern theological implications, nor judgments on "orthodox" and "heterodox" theologies, will be made. The only focus of this portion is an attempt to describe the structures of belief held by the earliest Christians as recorded by our earliest source: Paul.

Paul has much to say about the Old Testament and his belief in God in the seven undisputed Pauline letters. His letter to the church at Rome, however, contains the largest amount of doctrinal teaching, as Paul did not found the church there. It is not known who originally established the church. It is thought to have been started by some Jews who were present at Pentecost and returned to Rome with the gospel. If this conjecture is true, then one of the original disciples passed the gospel to a group of Jews, who founded the church themselves. Paul himself explains how he has not visited or had any contact with the church when he states that word of the faith at Rome has spread all over the world (Romans 1:8), and that he may, after many failed attempts, finally be able to visit the church to "impart... some spiritual gift" and "have a harvest" (Romans 1:10-13). This statement implies that he has not been able to make the visit there yet, but that he has heard about them.

Looking at Paul's introduction to his letter to Rome reinforces our earlier contention that distance led to the inability to consult the experts (i.e. the original apostles) and, thus, made local interpretation (and, inevitably and consequentially, divergence from the original message) a necessity. Paul apparently had wished and attempted to visit Rome or contact the church in some way for an extended period of time, but was unable to do so for multiple unnamed reasons. We have also examined the "gospel" preached by Paul and concluded that it left much open to extrapolation and little information about how to deal with everyday life. Thus, with distance making it impossible for Paul to visit Rome, it is easy to imagine conflict about theological issues emerging in the Roman church, especially as local converts were added to the church, since Rome was the seat of pagan religion.

Any contentions between Jews and Gentiles could possibly have been further exacerbated by the purported exile of Jews from Rome by the emperor Claudius around the year 49 (as recorded by Acts 18:2 and the Roman historian Suetonius, yet omitted by the Jewish historian Josephus, making it unclear whether this exile actually happened). This exile would possibly have left Gentiles in charge of the church until Nero allowed Jews to return to the city some time after Claudius died in 54. While this is an uncertain event, one can picture the Jews returning back to their church from exile and discovering many changes, especially regarding food purity and circumcision laws (conveniently, two main issues upon which Jewish and pagan Christian converts disagreed, and issues addressed by Paul in his letters). Adding weight to our speculation, Paul warns the Romans to "watch out for those who cause divisions and put obstacles in your way that are contrary to the teaching you have learned" (Romans 16:17). This statement serves as further evidence for our contention about disagreements in the church and the development of regional theologies, as we saw with our discussion of Galatians. This division cannot simply be due to influence from Greco-Roman philosophies or religion. While this influence may have been an issue, especially regarding food sacrifices to "idols" (see I Corinthians 8), Paul explicitly adds to his warning the statement that "such people are not serving our Lord Christ" (Romans 16:18). Here, Paul clearly points out that individuals had been teaching about Jesus or claiming to serve Jesus, but were presenting different teachings than his own (or, assumedly, those of the original Apostles). This warning echoes his description of the proponents of different Christianities, accused of trying to "pervert the Gospel," as we have already encountered in our analysis.

If the gospel was taught to the church at Rome, second-hand through the Jews who heard the message in Jerusalem, the Roman church already had a deficiency in foundational knowledge and instruction, as no original follower of Jesus was present to educate the infant church for any period of time. This is a possible reason for Paul's lengthy explanation of theology in his letter to the Romans. Furthermore, the degree of care that Paul takes in referencing Jesus to Judaism and Jewish history serves as evidence for our conjecture that Jews founded the Roman church. As a result, the letter to the Romans will make up the majority of our analysis about the earliest Christians' view on the Old Testament.

It is very obvious from Paul's address to the church at Rome that he has drawn no distinction between Yahweh, the Jewish

God, Creator of the earth and of mankind, and the God who sent Jesus to earth. Often what is not said is just as informative as what is. That these deities are not one and the same is an issue that Paul never even considers. Since Paul himself was a Jew, if he had believed that he had adopted another religion, he would have had to explain to the Jews at Rome how that religion was superior to or more truthful than Judaism. Instead, as we have previously mentioned, and will explore more deeply, Paul places his message about Jesus' death and resurrection, his "gospel," completely into the context of Judaism. This inclusion of the gospel into a Jewish framework makes it clear that he assumes that the God of Abraham and the God of Jesus is the same God, without even considering another possibility.

In his letter to Rome, Paul creates a continuum, describing Jewish religious history as pointing toward the coming of Jesus. Beginning with a description of mankind's sinfulness and conscious decision to ignore God (Romans 1:18-2:12), Paul quickly turns the argument to the Jewish law. Paul points to the law as demonstrating mankind's need for salvation from being under sin, since, according to Paul, "no one will be declared righteous in [God's] sight by observing the law; rather, through the law we become conscious of sin" (Romans 3:20). Paul points back to Abraham, believed to be the father of the Jewish people and religion, as an example of "justification" (uprightness in God's sight) by faith. This justification occurred outside of the law, since, according to Jewish theology, God did not reveal his law until Moses received it after bringing the Israelites out of Egypt (see Exodus). Paul subtly makes this point by explaining how God credited Abraham with righteousness before his circumcision (Romans 4:10-11). He openly makes this point again in Galatians 3:16-17:

The promises were spoken to Abraham and his seed... What I mean is this: The law, introduced 430 years later, does not set aside the covenant previously established by God... (i.e. righteousness by faith, as Paul states in Galatians 3:6).

According to Paul's argument, people such as Abraham could once be justified by faith. The law then illuminates sins and points to the need for and practice of sacrifices to atone for sins, but to a standard that none can meet. He then addresses how Jesus' death and resurrection solves this inherent problem of righteousness by giving a way to be justified by faith again:

For what the (Jewish) law was powerless to do in that it was weakened by the sinful nature, God did by sending his own Son in the likeness of sinful man to be a sin offering. And so he condemned sin in sinful man, in order that the righteous requirements of the law might be fully met in us... And if the spirit of him who raised Jesus from the dead is living in you, he who raised Christ from the dead will also give life to your mortal bodies through his Spirit, who lives in you. (Romans 8:3-4, 11).

Notice here that his gospel, at its core, is the same message as the one found in the creed of I Corinthians 15:1-8: that Jesus died for the sins of mankind and was raised by God. The only addition to Paul's "gospel" is not grouped with this declaration, but is his statement, much earlier in the letter, that he preached in his gospel that God will judge mankind through Jesus (Romans 2:16). Additionally, Paul changes his presentation to include terms such as "law" and "sin offering," which were directed solely at Jewish converts and served to further his seating of the gospel in the context of Judaism.

Paul spends the remainder of his letter discussing what to do after accepting this justification offered by the gospel of Jesus, and addressing other issues of the church. He provides some of the teaching and instructional foundation that the church should have received, had one of the original apostles been present for any period of time at Rome, when the church was in its infancy. This is not the issue we are addressing, and is where this analysis will stop. Clearly, however, Paul's theology, and, by extension, the theology of the earliest followers of Christ, made no distinction between the Old Testament God and the God of Jesus.

Restored View of God

When I consider the question of reconciling the character of the God of the Old Testament and the God of Jesus, I think about the movie *Bruce Almighty*, starring Jim Carrey and Morgan Freeman. Bruce (Jim Carrey) is a discontented news reporter who feels singled out by God after a series of bad turns in his career. The reality of his circumstances was that his selfish and negative attitude caused the majority of his problems, but he chose to blame God instead. In retaliation, Bruce lashes out at God, screaming, "Smite me, oh mighty smiter!" and claiming he could do a better job of running things. God (played by Morgan Freeman) responds to these claims by letting Bruce be God, with all of God's powers. Bruce proceeds to get back at a group of thugs who beat him up, to make news events happen so he can get exclusive coverage no matter what the consequences, and to ruin the career of his top competitor for the TV anchor job. Basically, Bruce uses his newly given power to benefit himself. When the prayers of all the people get to Bruce, he simply decides to respond "yes" to everything they request, like a Santa Claus without limits or a bad parent who spoils the children to get them to shut up.

So why am I bringing up this movie at this time, and what does the movie have to do with the questions posed in this chapter? Described above, when Bruce first gets God's powers, we get a snapshot of what an arrogant, prideful, self-centered and vengeful God would be like and how he would respond. In fact, one of the things we find out about Bruce is that he was completely selfish, even before he was given God's power. His selfishness ultimately loses him his girlfriend - and now I come to the second point. Bruce's first response when his girlfriend leaves is to "command" her to love him. However, it doesn't work, because it is in the very nature of love that it is freely given from the heart. God has told Bruce that he can't mess with anyone's free will, and in this scene, for the first time, Bruce begins to see the difficulties inherent in that instruction. In a deep depression, he asks God, "How do you make people love you without affecting free will?" God smiles and responds, "Welcome to my world, son. If you come up with an answer to that one, let me know."

As we read the Old Testament, we must read it first and foremost through the understanding that God is relating to a people to whom He has given free will. He will not "make" them, beginning with the story in the Garden of Eden where He does not control the choice of Adam and Eve to eat the fruit of the tree of knowledge of good and evil. According to this story in Genesis 3, God instructed Adam and Eve not to eat of the tree of knowledge of good and evil, and that they would surely die if they did. If it was His will that they know good and evil, He would not have instructed them in this way. Yet, they in their God-given free will took that knowledge into themselves anyway, and sin came into the world. The consequences of that choice are chronicled throughout the remainder of the Old Testament stories, and culminate in the cross of Christ.

There are numerous other Old Testament stories where the free will choice of the people involved results in consequences, some of which are far-reaching. However, I will focus on only two such stories here. The first I want to mention is from the story of Abraham, Isaac, and Jacob. As told in Genesis, the story of Abraham describes how God promised Abraham (then Abram) that he would be the father of a great nation, and that he and his wife Sarai would have a child in their old years. Nevertheless, neither Abram nor Sarai were inclined to wait on the Lord. Despairing of ever having a child of her own, Sarai encouraged Abram to conceive with her Egyptian servant, Hagar. In spite of that choice, Genesis 21:1 states, "Now the Lord was gracious to Sarah as He had said, and the Lord did for Sarah what He had promised." When the promised son Isaac was born, Sarah wanted Hagar and her son Ishmael gone, so Abraham sent them away. According to the story, God tells Abraham that, *according to his original promise,* "I will make the son of the maidservant into a nation also, because he is your offspring (Genesis 21:13)." Later, Isaac's son, Jacob, also has a problem with his brother, Esau. Esau ultimately marries foreign women, and his lineage and that of Ishmael cross. From this lineage, the people arise who will be the long-standing enemies of Israel, and from whom they must take the Promised Land. This is one story that shows the long-term and far-reaching consequences of the choice of one man not to follow the will of God.

The second story I want to discuss is how Israel first received a king. According to I Samuel 8, the elders of Israel went to Samuel and asked him to appoint a king to lead them. This request "displeased Samuel (I Samuel 8:6)," so he prayed and God told him, "it is not you they have rejected, but they have rejected me as their king (I Samuel 8:7)." According to the story, God told Samuel that their rejection of Him was nothing new, having been the case since they were brought out of slavery in Egypt (This comment highlights God's patience with the "stiff-necked" people of Israel). God tells Samuel to warn the people of Israel about all that a king will do to them, and Samuel outlines to the people the many terrible consequences of their choice, concluding with the warning, "When that day comes, you will cry out for relief from the king you have chosen, and the Lord will not answer you in that day (I Samuel 8:18)." But the people didn't listen to the warnings, instead saying they wanted a king to lead them and fight their battles, so Samuel repeated what they had said to God. God responded, "Listen to them and give them a king (I Samuel 8:22)." Of course, what God had warned did happen, and throughout I and II Kings and I and II Chronicles, we read about the actions of the kings of Israel, a few of them good kings but most of them dreadful, leading the people farther and farther away from God and ultimately into captivity. Yet, in spite of that choice, from the line of King David, God would bring the salvation of the world.

"Wait," you may be saying right now, "didn't you just finish a chapter about not looking at the Bible as representing actual historical events word for word?" This is true, but our analysis is not discussing whether Adam and Eve actually lived in a garden and walked around with a physical manifestation of God and had kids who suddenly found women to marry even though there were only four people on the earth. We are not even suggesting one way or the other if the discourse between Samuel, God, and the Israelites happened. We are looking at these stories of God across the Bible as how they represent the character of God, and attempting to point out whether the events recorded actually happened or not is irrelevant. Rather, the focus is on what the stories say about God's character, and whether or not *this* remains stable and consistent.

These, and many other stories like them, show the character of God as the Redeemer. He does not prevent bad choices, nor does He prevent the consequences of those bad choices from happening. For example, Israel was taken captive into Babylon as a *consequence* of their rejection of God as their king and leader, following foreign gods and worshipping idols. According to Deuteronomy 28 through 30, Moses outlined the consequences that would come, both from choosing to love God ("life and prosperity," verse 30:15) and from choosing to abandon God ("death and destruction," verse 30:15). In spite of these warnings, the people of Israel opted to reject God, and the consequences of that choice play out. Moses tells the people, "what I am commanding you today is not too difficult for you or beyond your reach…No, the word is very near you; it is in your mouth and in your heart so you may obey it (Deuteronomy 30:11)." Paul quotes from this section of the Old Testament (Romans 10:6-10) to describe the righteousness that comes by faith in Christ. Ultimately then, the consequences of the choices of the people of Israel were redeemed by God in Jesus.

To me, the Old Testament stories are not about a vengeful and arrogant God. They are a series of stories that portray the willingness of God to offer chance after chance to a people who reject Him. While He allows the consequences of their choices to come to fruition, He repeatedly invites them back to Him, brings them out of captivity and takes them back as His people. Finally, His love is displayed in His choice to take the sin on Himself. I will speak more about His ultimate choice later in this chapter.

Supporting this restored understanding of the character of God as the redeemer is the nature of Jesus. As noted earlier, Paul describes Jesus as humble and meek, and by His nature a servant. Paul also expresses directly that the nature of God is in the love of Christ:

> Who shall separate us from the love of Christ?... I am convinced that neither death nor life, neither angels nor demons, neither the present nor the future, nor any powers, neither height nor depth, nor anything else in all creation, will be able to separate us *from the love of God that is in Christ Jesus our Lord.* (Romans 8:35, 38-39, italics added for emphasis)

If it is true, as discussed in the historical section of this chapter, that the earliest Christians believed that God of the Old Testament and the God of Jesus were the same God, and that He did not suddenly change His character at Christ's birth or His death and resurrection, then God is, and always has been, humble and meek with the nature of a servant. God's character is, and always has been, love and grace (Romans 5:1-2). This picture is quite a contrast to the proud, arrogant, condemning god who demands our praise and crushes us at every sin.

What I would like to do now is to briefly go back through a few Old Testament stories about God's relationships with some of His chosen partners, specifically to assess this nature I am describing. There were many individuals that God selected as partners, from Adam to Abraham, from Moses to David, from Solomon to Esther. Which of these people was perfect, without sin? We often make the mistake of trying to divide the characters in the stories of the Old Testament into good guys and bad guys. However, in reality, they were all human, complete with human frailties and foibles. As I have said many times to my Sunday school class, "them is us" (Please forgive the "southernism" here). Abraham, the Father of the people of God who received the first covenant promises, lied about his wife being his sister to save himself, allowing Pharaoh in Egypt to "take her in" (Genesis 12). Moses, the great Bringer of the Law, argued with God, whined and complained, wheedled and justified to try to get out of his calling, then *after* witnessing the great miracles of God's salvation, listened to the people and brought up water by his own power (Exodus). David, the man chosen to bear the lineage of the Son of God, lusted after his neighbor's wife, slept with her, and then got the man killed to cover the adultery (II Samuel 11).

Yet, in spite of all of these human sins, God loved these people. He cherished them and made promises to them, and He partnered with them to accomplish what needed to be done for His people. Could God have freed all of Israel from Egypt without Moses, with a bolt of lightning from the sky that simply destroyed Egypt? He is God, so yes He *could*. But He didn't. More significantly, He wouldn't. He even gave the Egyptian Pharaoh multiple opportunities to listen to Him without major consequences (have you ever wondered why there were *ten* plagues, and not just one *big* one? This is, again, a representation of the character of God). As the story explains, He chose instead, from His character of humility and service and His nature of love, to allow His creation to have authority, to give His children the choice to love Him and to partner with Him, and to credit their faith as righteousness even in the midst of their sin and weakness (Romans 4:3, 4:9, 4:16, 5:6-8).

The covenant of Christ is not a "new" covenant in the sense that it was a new concept or idea. In other words, God didn't change His mind, or His nature. It is the culmination of the covenant with Abraham. Our faith (in Christ) is credited to us as righteousness. As Paul states, "This righteousness from God comes through faith in Christ Jesus to all who believe (Romans 3:22)."

What about God's wrath? Don't the Old Testament and Paul both talk about God's wrath? Paul writes in Romans, in the context of explaining to the Jews how the Gentiles, who were not the chosen people of God, could come to be saved:

> It does not, therefore, depend on man's desire or effort, but on God's mercy…What if God, choosing to show His wrath and make His power known, bore with great patience the objects of His wrath-prepared for destruction? What if He did this to make the riches of His glory known to the objects of His mercy…" What then shall we say? That the Gentiles, who did not pursue righteousness, have obtained it, a righteousness that is by faith; but Israel, who pursued a law of righteousness, has not attained it. Why not? Because they pursued it not by faith but as if it were by works. (Romans 9:30-32).

In other words, God chose to put up with the depravity and sin of the Gentiles with patience, and to offer them a path to salvation, in order to show the Jews and the Gentiles the operation of His great love, grace, and mercy, so that the Jews could see that they did not and could not save themselves through the keeping of the law. God did this out of His love for all of His creation, for, as we have discussed, His very nature is love.

I contend, then, that God's wrath is directed toward sin; it has been, is, and will be poured out against sin. God, the loving Father, is angry over what sin has done in and to His children. He has witnessed throughout history the consequences of sin destroying His people, more than once bringing them into captivity, darkening their eyes to any remembrance of Him, hardening their hearts, and creating their suffering and death. This was not His will. The truth of His will is revealed in the story of Eden before the introduction of sin. The consequences of the choice of sin were many, including death and exile from Eden, for to live forever in a state of sin was too cruel and awful to consider. But, I reiterate, this was not God's will.

God chose, then, to redeem the choice of man to sin by taking the sin onto Himself, through Christ on the cross. While our concept of justice might be described as "whoever sins pays the price," God's idea of justice is love, exemplified in Jesus, which is, "you sin and I will pay the price." On the cross, he removed the consequences of sin from us, took them on and suffered for us, and restored the opportunity to have an intimate relationship with Him to us, as He intended all along.

Through Christ, God has restored to us the opportunity to choose His original will: to choose life, to choose freedom from sin through faith in Christ, and to choose to partner again with Him in intimate relationship. Paul describes this in Romans 5:5; "...God has poured out His love into our hearts by the Holy Spirit, whom He has given us." Again, as in the last chapter, we see God's intention: that we know Him and His love for us through the presence of His Holy Spirit in our hearts.

A distorted or perverted view of God is a hindrance that interferes with our ability to live in that partnership with God. Go back for a moment to the introduction of this chapter, and the discussion of God as the police officer and God as Santa Claus. I want you to think for a moment about how you feel and respond to a police officer when the blue lights are flashing in your rear view mirror. Even if you have done nothing wrong, don't you feel a twinge of shame and a cold grip of fear on your heart? Isn't there a sense of, "Oh *no!*" where you wish above all you could just get out of there unscathed?

Now try to remember back to your child-like view of Santa Claus. Many children are quite afraid to sit in Santa's lap at the mall. My husband has shared with me his own terror as a child over being "that close to someone who wielded such power." What "power" did Santa hold over him? The answer can be found in the capricious and conditional nature of Santa's "presents." We all know the song, "You better watch out, you better not cry, you better not pout, I'm telling you why…he knows if you've been bad or good, so be good for goodness sake." One slipup, and the omniscient semi-deity that evolved from legends about a saint would refuse to lavish his gifts unto you, and Christmas morning would be ruined. The horror of it! On the other hand, what if you believed you had been a good little boy or girl? What comes to my mind is Sally in "A Charlie Brown Christmas," making her list of yearly demands, then at Charlie Brown's apparent dismay, justifying her greed by saying, "All I want is what I have coming to me. All I want is my fair share." Santa Claus owed her! This sounds a lot like the church's current view of prayer to me.

In addition, Santa is the quintessential mystery man: the once-a-year visitor in the night who rains gifts down the chimney (from above), and you never hear from him again until the next year. In fact, as the American legend tells it, if you happened to be awake when he came he would pass you by, so desperately did he want to remain unseen.

Do you see the commonality in these images?

The commonality is *distance.* God, viewed in this way, is "up and out there," always "safely" detached and remote, always a mystery to us. The last thing you want is intimacy with a police officer (assuming of course he or she is not your spouse!), and

Santa Claus is only as valued as what you can get out of him. God is neither the Punisher nor Santa Claus. He is not prideful or arrogant, demanding or harsh, condemning or cruel; neither is He a manipulator nor someone to be manipulated.

Let's revisit "Bruce Almighty" for just a moment more. First, we get to witness what happens when a god-like power is selfish and prideful. In Bruce, we get to glimpse a reflection of God as vigilante and God as Santa. But, when Bruce realizes that he can't make his girlfriend love him, he is humbled and realizes his love for her above all else. God asks Bruce what he wants. "Grace. You want her back?" Out of his newfound humility, Bruce responds, "No. I want her to be happy, no matter what that means. I want her to find someone who will treat her with all the love she deserved from me. I want her to meet someone who will see her always as I do now, through Your eyes." God answers, "Now *that's* a prayer." I agree. It is that kind of love that God wants to share with us.

So I suggest to you that, if you have viewed God in these ways or you have heard it taught that God has any of these qualities, those beliefs may be a part of what keeps you from truly seeing and knowing Him. I encourage you to dismiss any such images from your mind, and to genuinely ask Jesus to show you Who God really is, through the love of the Holy Spirit in your heart. I believe this question is one of two vital questions we *must* know the answer to in order to have true freedom in our hearts and a deep, experiential relationship with God.

Chapter 4

Can God Be Known?

The Current State of the Church and the Mystery of God

I SUPPOSE I ALWAYS WAS, AND STILL AM, ONE OF THOSE PEOPLE who feel the need to understand. In math classes, my teachers would say, "OK, here you add three, then multiply." I would raise my hand and ask, "Why?" Typically, they would respond, "Because that is how you work it." I was hard-headed enough to be persistent, but the teacher, more often than not, did not explain the "why" and I was left frustrated. My husband calls this notion, "The pulling numbers out of thin air theory of math." Clearly, math was not his favorite subject!

On those rare occasions when I had a teacher who was willing to explain why, I was like a dehydrated wanderer in the desert who had found an oasis. Suddenly, light bulbs would go off, concepts would become comprehensible, and I would have an "aha!" moment. However, I eventually came to understand two things from this exasperating process. First, I realized that many of the teachers didn't know the answers to the "why" questions themselves, and that the most likely reason they would not answer my questions was because they could not. Second, I generalized from those experiences where concepts were explained to me that things did indeed make sense, that there was a reason why and it was even a good thing to seek the answer, and that if I grasped a concept in the big picture I retained the material as part of an overall understanding. In other words, if I understood why, I internalized the concepts.

Psychology teaches that there are two processes of how we adapt in order to learn: assimilation and accommodation. Assimilation is loosely defined as bringing new ideas and concepts into an already existing pattern of understanding (called a schema). In order to assimilate, the new concept either has to fit the existing schema, or has to be altered or molded to fit the existing schema. Accommodation is loosely defined as creating a new pattern of understanding in order to retain new information that does not or cannot fit into any existing schema. Of the two, assimilation is the easiest and the one preferred by human beings. If there is any possible way to make new data fit into an existing pattern, we'll do it, even if it means squeezing size 10 feet into a size 7 pair of shoes. The Body of Christ is no different in its desire to assimilate rather than accommodate information.

There are many ways to assimilate new ideas. I can alter my perception of the new information to make it fit. I can compartmentalize incongruent information into two separate schemas and never let the two concepts come into contact with each other. I can get mad and reject the new idea completely. I can use questionable logic or ignore certain elements of the new data. Or, the method addressed in this chapter, I can simply accept that it does not make sense, believe that it doesn't have to make sense, and call it a "mystery." When faced with a difficult truth or a concept that seems to contradict well-established dogma and assumed or accepted convention, the church has employed all of these devices to assimilate rather than accommodate the thorny or opposing beliefs.

Often, in my many years as a part of the Body of Christ, I feel like a student raising her hand to ask "why" and hearing "because that is just how it is." I have also found that if I go on to explain the reason for my question (for example, if I point out illogic or incongruence), the most likely response is, "God is a mystery," or, "There are just some mysteries of God that we will never understand." The "mystery" statement will then be followed often by a quick subject change or a lot of language about having faith. Furthermore, the people who are responding in this way believe their response is Scriptural. It is my experience that this idea is quite prevalent in the current Christian church.

I have drawn the same conclusion about church theology that I did about math teachers: members of the body cannot answer the "why" questions so they use the "mystery" response as their failsafe, default position. In addition, I believe God's truth does make sense, it is OK that I want to know why, and the more I understand, the more I will be able to internalize in my heart, retain and apply.

Unfortunately, history is replete with the consequences of faulty assimilation in the church, from the earliest development of whole new theologies like Gnosticism or Marcionism to explain elements of faith the newly formed churches did not understand, to divisive disagreements about circumcision and food laws. No wonder Paul warned so severely against any gospel other than the one the people heard from him.

Historical Analysis

Did Paul and the original Christians believe that the character of God was an unsolvable mystery, shrouded in secrecy?

Did they view God as a being that they should simply accept on faith and not try to understand? In order to discuss this issue, we must first understand the meaning of the word "mystery." Today, to most people, the word commonly means "something that is difficult or impossible to understand or explain," or "secrecy or obscurity," or "a novel, play, or film dealing with a puzzling crime." These are the first three entries under "mystery" in the Oxford English Dictionary, and also what comes to most people's minds when they hear the word. It is vital to the understanding of the theology of the earliest Christians to understand the terminology they employed. In order to understand the terminology, we must analyze the historical context in which Paul wrote.

Paul was born in Tarsus, a city in modern-day Turkey, into a Hellenized Jewish culture; that is, followers of Judaism who, due to Greek colonization and influence, adopted various aspects of the Greek culture, alphabet, language, or philosophy.[13] We have previously discussed how the early Christians might have incorporated aspects of the local culture, religion, or philosophy in order to develop their own theologies and deal with issues unanswered by Paul's gospel. This was not a singular occasion. Cultural borrowings occur wherever societies come into contact with one another. Sometimes one culture is dominant and assimilates the submissive culture into its own, and sometimes there is simply mutual adoption from both cultures; while each retains its own distinctive cultural identity, aspects of either culture diffuse within the other.[14] This process was actually recognized as a problem by ancient writers. An example of ancient attitudes toward cultural borrowing comes from the book of I Maccabees, which is accepted as Old Testament canon by Catholic and Orthodox religions, but seen as apocryphal by Protestants (Even today, Christianities are not using the same Bible!). I Maccabees describes how Greek occupation led to the defilement of Jewish religion and law and the adoption of Greek culture, notably the *gymnasium*, one of the main Greek cultural centers.

Even after the establishment of an "independent" Jewish "kingdom" under the Romans, Greek was still the *lingua franca* (the primary language) of the educated Jews. Tying this historical context back in with Paul's Hellenization and his writing, every text that was compiled to make the New Testament was written in Greek, and thus all of Paul's letters were written in Greek. This is not to say that Paul adopted all aspects of Greek culture into his Jewish life. However, he definitely employed the Greek language when writing his letters. This is not only because Paul, having been born into a Hellenized city in Asia Minor, probably grew up speaking Greek as his first language, but also because it was the most widely understood language of the region, and when writing letters to be read aloud to an audience, he would want to be understood.

When one learns a language, either as a primary tongue or when one becomes fluent enough in a secondary language, he or she begins thinking in the terms of that language. For example, if a person who speaks English wishes to learn Spanish effectively, he or she begins by translating the Spanish vocabulary into English and making translated versions of sentences in his or her head, before reciting the newly formed Spanish sentences. With enough practice, the person will eventually progress to an association of the Spanish word with a mental conception of the object or idea he or she wishes to describe, in the same way the primary language, English, is processed. This procession will change from "*mesa* means 'table,'" which calls up the mental image of a table, to "*mesa*" immediately calling up the image in the person's mind. Even the newly popularized *Rosetta Stone* computer language program claims on its website to have higher efficacy because it "reconnects people to the language skills they used successfully to master their first language." The program works by associating pictures with words, so that there is "absolutely no translation or memorization to hold you back." Thus, it attempts to begin immediately the mental association between objects and the new words for them. This process allows a person to begin thinking in that language, much the same way Paul thought in Greek.

When Paul used the Greek language, he employed vocabulary in a Greek context and with Greek meaning, because he thought in Greek. As such, an understanding of the Greek meaning of "mystery" must now be discussed. In Greek, and in Greek culture, cults known as "mystery religions" were prevalent. These cults (such as the Eleusinian mysteries) consisted of initiation ceremonies in which initiates took part in a reenactment of a mythological story (such as the goddess Demeter's search for her abducted daughter Persephone), in order to learn the story of the events and the rituals, which the other members knew and understood.[15] Thus, the idea of a "mystery" related more to a revelation of an event, or to a religious knowledge that was given to its members, rather than an unsolvable puzzle. Therefore, it is likely that Paul employed the word in its Greek context to explain concepts that were revealed to and understood by members of the Christian faith. This ancient meaning is even preserved by the continued entry under "mystery" in the Oxford English Dictionary, as "the secret rites of an ancient or tribal religion" and "a religious belief based on divine revelation."

Now, I am not saying that Christianity was an adoption of Greek mystery religions, since Paul freely preached his gospel to whomever would listen and wherever he went, and did not withhold his information only for initiates. Nor am I saying that Paul agreed with later Gnostic doctrine and held that only certain people could understand the true secret *gnosis* of God and would be allowed to the highest level of heaven, and that all other initiates and followers of the religion do not understand the truth. Instead, he claims, "For since the creation of the world God's invisible qualities – his eternal power and divine nature – have been clearly seen, being understood from what has been made... (Romans 1:20)." I am only explaining that the context of the Greek word *mysterion* meant something different to a first century Greek and Hellenized Jewish audience than "mystery" does to most people today.

The actual Greek word *mysterion* occurs within the undisputed Pauline letters only three times: twice in Romans and once in I Corinthians. In order to provide evidence for our previous conclusion: that Paul used the Greek word with the Greek contextual meaning in mind, we will look at the way he uses the word in the context of his writing. Romans 11:25 states "I do not want you to be ignorant of this *mystery*, brothers, so that you may not be conceited: Israel has experienced a hardening in part until the full number of the Gentiles has come in (italics added for emphasis)." In this writing, Paul explains a piece of information to his "brothers," fellow Christians, regarding the inclusion of Gentile converts into the Israelite faith. Similarly, in Romans 16:25-26, Paul sends greetings:

> "[T]o him who is able to establish you by my gospel and the proclamation of Jesus Christ, according to the revelation of the *mystery* hidden for long ages past, but now revealed and made known through the prophetic writings by the command of the eternal God, so that all nations might believe and obey him." (italics added)

This greeting clearly explains Paul's concept of "mystery" as revelation. Finally, in I Corinthians 15:51, Paul explains the resurrection of the dead, saying, "Listen, I tell you a *mystery*: We will not all sleep, but we will all be changed... (italics added)." Here, Paul himself reveals the piece of information to the Christians in Corinth.

It should be clear by this analysis alone that Paul meant "mystery" in a Greek context, as a revelation. However, even in the disputed Pauline letters, "mystery" means revelation. In Ephesians, a letter of questionable, though not rejected, Pauline authorship, "mystery" is used six times (a point of contention about the actual authorship, since Paul rarely employs the word in his undisputed letters: three times in seven letters). In each case, Ephesians 1:9, 3:3, 3:4, 3:6, 3:9, and 6:19, the word is used in the sense of revelation. Additionally, in Colossians, another letter of disputed authorship, the word appears four times: Colossians 1:26, 1:27, 2:2, and 4:3, referring to revelation in each instance. The word also appears in I Timothy 3:16 and in Revelation 1:20, 10:7, 17:5, and 17:7. All of these verses, with the exception of Revelation 17:5, where the word is in a symbolic title, explain mystery as revelation. I will not describe here in detail each verse and its full context, since these letters are not part of Paul's undisputed teaching. However, I have listed them, so that you, as a reader, may research this usage yourself and discover on your own that not only Paul, but also other early Christians, employed *mysterion* in the Greek context to mean something revealed.

Restored Understanding of the Revelation of God

From the historical analysis, it is my hope that you can see that, for Paul and other early Christians, the "mystery" of God was the revelation of God through Christ. Christ has come;

God has been revealed in Him. Basically, then, the use (or should I say, misuse?) of the "mystery" argument to allow for assimilation of incongruent and illogical ideas in Christian belief is itself based on a false premise. In the nature, character and teachings of Christ we see a reflection of the nature, character and truth of God.

Does that mean that there is nothing left beyond our understanding?

Many of you who are reading this chapter will assume that I am about to explore all the elements of God and His truth that are still unrevealed, still to be explained to us. "OK," you could be thinking, "Good. Now she will agree that there are still mysteries. She will call it something else, and maybe explain it in a different way, but here we go; I am now ready to assimilate!"

My answer is, "Yes, that is what it means. There is nothing left that is beyond our understanding." Oops. The assimilation button is on pause. Now what?

I am more of a fan of *Star Trek* than a fan of *Star Trek: the Next Generation* (the "mystery" of my age is probably revealed in this fact); however, TNG (as it is known to Trekkies) had its moments that I appreciated. One such moment was a series of really interesting shows about an alien race called the Borg. The Borg were a collective, working like the functioning of a beehive; all Borg were connected to each other and they operated as one entity. Unfortunately for the crew of the Enterprise, this collective consciousness made the Borg virtually unbeatable. The Borg were like locusts, with one exception: rather than just wiping out other species, they would bring a number of the alien race into the collective, and only destroy the ones who would resist. The Borg had two sayings that they repeated each time they met a new individual, group or race: "You will be assimilated. Resistance is futile." The end result was the same as a locust plague, of course; the alien race was extinguished completely, because once an individual became a part of the collective, he or she lost all sense of individuality, and the ability to think of anything beyond the "whole" was gone. This is great allegory, and there are many wonderful metaphors in this series of episodes. However, for this chapter, I want to focus on only one concept: assimilation. The way the Borg handled assimilation was either you became a part of the collective or you were destroyed. I would like to use the Borg assimilation process as an analogy for how the church evaluates challenging ideas.

I was in a Bible study of Galatians, and for this particular class we were focusing on chapters 2 and 3 of the letter. The discussion, as you might expect if you are familiar with this section of Galatians, went to the question of the law. The teacher pointed out several verses in this section that indicate we have attained redemption from the law in Christ (Galatians 3:13-14), that before Christ we were "held prisoners by the law until faith should be revealed (Galatians 3:23)," that the law cannot give life (Galatians 3:22), that we are justified by faith alone (Galatians 2:15-3:7, 3:24), and that we are "no longer under the supervision of the law (Galatians 3:25)." Many in the class struggled with these ideas, indicating by their arguments that they believed they were still under the law and they enjoyed the security of being able to gain at least God's approval, if not salvation, through their actions. The teacher pointed to confrontational words of Paul in the beginning of Galatians 3, and reiterated that justification cannot be obtained through their own effort. Round and round, and back and forth the discussion went, until someone relieved the class of this struggle by saying a version of the infamous "mystery" quote: "I guess we are not meant to fully understand this mystery of God."

We went on to finish the rest of Chapter 3 (verses 26-29), which, although it reiterates and confirms Paul's earlier declaration of justification through faith in Christ by stating that we are "all sons of God through faith in Christ Jesus (Galatians 3:26)," brought no struggle or disagreement from the class. The class settled into a comfortable complacency, missing the central point of the last three verses because they accepted instead the statement that this issue was part of that undefined "mystery" of God. They were off the hook, and relieved to be there.

This response effectively "destroyed" the concepts the teacher was trying to present. At that point, since the proposal of freedom from the law would not "be assimilated" into the collective viewpoint, and since we simply had to accept that we couldn't understand this "mystery," the ideas were hit with a "disruptor beam" and blasted out of the way. The conversation ended, and so ended the opportunity for growth and change. Translated into Borg, they were saying, "You will be assimilated. Resistance is futile." Their disruptor beam had destroyed the conceptual species. How am I so certain the concepts were destroyed? We had a "sentence" prayer at the end of the lesson, and the person sitting next to me (who had not taken a position in the discussion) prayed, "Lord, help us to better keep your law."

The church's handy category of the "mystery" of God allows for completely contradictory ideas to coexist. It permits compartmentalization of theology into contrasting aspects such that we can even allow ourselves to include characteristics of Satan as part of God's nature. It justifies our assimilation of God into our worldly view. After all, if I am more comfortable with the idea of being under the supervision of the law, or having a say in my own justification through my own effort, then that point of view must be true, right?

However, (and I want to emphasize this point) **God will not be assimilated.**

Paul's teachings make it clear that, instead, we are to **accommodate** for God. Romans 12:2 states, "Do not conform any longer to the pattern of this world, but be transformed by the renewing of your mind. Then you will be able to test and approve what God's will is – His good, pleasing and perfect will." If I restated the first half of this verse using the language of learning and adaptation, it would go something like this: "Do not keep assimilating ideas into the existing schemas you have accepted from this world, but accommodate, allowing new schemas to be created in your mind by God." In I Corinthians 3:18-19, Paul makes the same point in a different way: "Do not deceive yourselves. If any one of you thinks he is wise by the standards of this age, he should become a 'fool' so that he may become wise. For the wisdom of this world is foolishness in God's sight."

So how do we restore these early teachings to the foundations of our beliefs? First, we need to see "mystery" as Paul saw mystery, the Hellenized meaning as the revelation of God. We need to adopt an attitude of *expectation* that we can and will understand God's truth. Then, realizing that the mystery of God is revealed in Christ, we need to be willing to move outside our comfort zones, seeking to know Christ anew, laying aside our accepted or preconceived doctrine (not "gospel" as discussed in previous chapters, but things such as denominational dogma) in exchange for new presentations through the Spirit of Christ of Who God is and who He says we are. We must drop our attempts to force God to assimilate into our worldly schemas. I encourage you to ask yourself if you are willing to let God shake up your worldview. Will you choose to allow the more difficult process of accommodation to take place in your heart and mind? As I have expressed to countless clients in my office, I don't want you to take my word for it. Instead, from a position of not knowing (no mandatory schemas with which the information must assimilate) and with a willingness to hear and see and be taught new things, ask the Lord for the truth. What you *experience* with Him can transform and renew your soul.

I will return to *Star Trek* for a glimpse into the accommodation process, this time pulling from the original series. In one episode, the Enterprise comes upon a hollow sphere hurtling on a collision course toward an inhabited planet. In order to save the people on the planet, a team goes to repair the damage to the mechanism that was controlling the course of the sphere and to reset the proper course. However, when Kirk, Spock and McCoy beam aboard, they find life forms inside the hollow sphere who take them captive. They discover that the people believe themselves to be on a planet, and the inside of the orb has been made to look like a planet, including a planetarium-like star show at "night" and sunlight during the "day," both projected on the dome inside the sphere. To complete the illusion and keep it intact, the population has been "given" a religious system, including beliefs about "sacred obedience" and "forbidden places." The "Temple of the Oracle" housed the damaged mechanism, so to repair it the crew must violate a sacred place. However, the Prime Directive (for those non-Trek folks, that is an order not to interfere with the normal development of other cultures/species/life forms) will not allow the Enterprise crew to tell the populace the truth about their situation. While they are trying to solve this difficult problem, an old man secretly comes to the crew and tells them of a time when he climbed a forbidden mountain. He then announces, his eyes gleaming with hidden knowledge, "Things are not as they teach us. For the world is hollow, and I have touched the sky!"

Over the years, this image (and statement) has become for me a symbol of both the process and the impact of accommodation. Having believed his whole life that he was on a planet's surface, it is his *experience of a new truth* that opens his eyes to a new reality.

Later in the episode, the high priestess of the Temple reveals to McCoy the hiding place of "the Book of the People" which contains all the things the people will need to know when they are given the "Promised New World." McCoy asks her, "Aren't you curious to know what is in the book?" "No," she responds, "It is enough for me to know we will receive all knowledge when we arrive." She believes what she has been taught without question or exploration, but this blind acceptance is going to destroy her "world" and millions of individuals on the inhabited planet in their path.

In desperation, Kirk tells the high priestess the truth about their "world" being a spaceship. Her struggle with the new information, which directly opposes everything she has always believed and based her entire life and vocation on, is best revealed in her angry response: "Why would the Creators keep us in darkness?" Not only does she *want* to reject what she is being told, she fears the punishment of the Oracle. But the question of the truth is now in her mind, and she decides she must seek the answer. In her struggle to "know the truth of the world," as she calls it, she asks the Oracle the same question ("Why would the Creators keep us in darkness?"), this time to try to understand the purpose in not revealing to the people that they were on a ship. This progression reveals the impact of accommodation; she has accepted a new paradigm for seeing her world and she is seeking a new schema to be formed from the new information. Kirk and Spock retrieve the book and open the altar of the Temple to reveal the drive system of the spacecraft, repair the system and restore the original course. McCoy invites the high priestess to come with him off the ship, but she refuses, saying she now understands the great plan and purpose of the Creators, to save their race, and that she will honor their purpose and go with the people to the new planet. Her accommodation is complete, but she decides not to tell the rest of the population the truth, since she believes they will not be able to accept it; they would be unable to accommodate the new ideas.

As I reflect on this story, I see many similarities between the "people" of the spaceship and the church. Their "theology" has them looking to a future "new world" for the revelation of all knowledge, similar to the Christian response in the face of a difficult question or contradictory concept, that the mystery of God will not be revealed until we reach heaven. Questioning certain doctrinal beliefs is "forbidden" at pain of punishment and fear of rejection. I believe there exists in the church a fear that exploration and accommodation might lead to chaos or abandonment of belief. It is as if the church supposes that the faith of the people is so fragile that this type of questioning would destroy it altogether. This fear was the guiding reason for the "Oracle" keeping hidden the true condition of the planet from all the people. Perhaps accommodation is seen as "sacrilege," as expressed by the high priestess. However, for the civilization in this particular *Star Trek* episode, the truth saved them from destruction.

Maybe the same would be true for the Church.

Chapter 5

Does God Make Sense?

The Current State of the Church on Logical Thought

In Chapter 4, we explored the processes of assimilation and accommodation, ways that our brains learn and adapt to new data. I want to focus now on the acceptance of illogical thinking and the use of distorted and twisted logic as means to continue to use assimilation of new information as opposed to accommodating for God.

At times it has seemed to me that the church sees intelligent logic as contrary to faith, almost as if reason does not exist in God's realm. Here are just a few examples of this lack of reason, using both verses of Scripture valued by the church and doctrine commonly taught in church:

1) According to the Lord's Prayer, Jesus taught us to pray for God's will to be done on earth as it is in heaven, indicating this is not already so. However, in spite of this instruction, we are taught that everything that happens is God's will.

2) According to what is traditionally called the Sermon on the Mount, in Matthew 6:19-21, Jesus says not to store up earthly treasures that can be stolen and destroyed but

to store up treasures in heaven, "for where your treasure is, there your heart will be also." At the same time, we are told that those who receive money and other riches on earth are especially blessed by God through His provision.

3) According to all Christian denominations, a central tenet of beliefs is stated in John 3:16, "For God so loved the world that He gave His one and only Son that *whoever* believes in Him shall not perish but have eternal life (italics added for emphasis)." However, some Christians also say that God destroys His own creation, by arbitrarily picking and choosing some of His own to be saved and some to be lost.

4) In a beloved story of Jesus' last night, as described in John 13:1-17, Jesus takes on the role of the lowest servant and washes His disciples' feet, an attitude reinforced in Philippians 2:5-7, which says, "Your attitude should be the same as that of Christ Jesus, who being in very nature God, did not consider equality with God something to be grasped, but made himself nothing, taking the very nature of a servant…" All the while frequent statements are being made from pulpits and in Christian books that Jesus *demands* our praise and worship, like an arrogant, prideful person in need of a self-esteem boost, or a spoiled child.

These examples above are just a few of many possible choices that I could use to illustrate the point that, in the current state of things in the church, illogical thinking is prevalent, and acceptable. I have tried to use central or basic church teaching, rather than treading into the realm of the extremes. But, there are denominations or groups of Christians out there who accept such bizarre ideas as, "I value life so much I am willing to kill an abortion doctor," or, "Jesus declared that his word should be spread to the four corners of the earth, therefore the earth is square," or, "once saved always saved, but if you ever sin, you are going straight to hell!"

Contradictions are not addressed. Opposing arguments are used simultaneously with no apparent difficulty. And we call this absence of reason, "faith."

Historical Analysis

When many people think of Greek culture and language, they immediately make the association with philosophy. Indeed, the foundations of Western philosophical thought owe their origins to the Greeks. From the first Milesian philosophers Thales, Anaximander, and Anaximenes (whom you might not have heard of), to other pre-Socratics such as Heraclitus, Xenophanes, and Parminedes, to Plato and Aristotle (whom you have most definitely heard of), the Greeks developed techniques and methods of philosophical thought, logic, inquiry, rhetoric, and argumentation that shaped the ideas of the Mediterranean world. Different philosophical schools of thought proposed varying views on understanding the universe, humanity and life, although all employed the same techniques and methods to argue their points of view. For example, the Skeptics believed gaining true knowledge was unattainable for man (not that truth was impossible, because that in itself would be a truth statement, only that knowledge of truth was impossible). Epicureans believed the gods were uninvolved in the affairs of man and that maximizing pleasure was the ultimate good (the Epicurean goal of *ataraxia* was not reckless hedonism, as many polemicists of the time wrote and most people today believe, but rather tranquility and freedom from fear through seeking modest pleasures with the minimum chance of pain. Thus, eating is pleasurable, but eating too much is painful, so eat in moderation; attaining pleasure but avoiding the later painful consequences of overindulgence). In contrast, the Stoics taught that reality was material and had a sense of order, *logos*; that a life lived by following reason, practicing self control, and being objective, made one free from passions (in the ancient sense of sufferings; i.e. the *Passion* of the Christ) and put one in harmony with the divine *logos* of the universe. Ultimately for a Stoic there was no significant difference between nature and God, since everything in nature was part of the *logos* (for Christian acceptance or reconciliation of Stoic patterns of thought, look at John 1 -- Jesus becomes the divine *logos*).[16]

The moral tenets of the Stoic school of philosophy were adopted by many notable Romans, including such celebrities as the Emperor Marcus Aurelius, Seneca the Younger, Cato the Younger, and Cicero, who was considered during his life and still by many today to be the premier rhetorician of all time and upon whose speeches and treatises we base our grammar for "classical" Latin (Cicero was not technically a Stoic, but he adhered to many of the moral teachings of the philosophy). The "Socratic method," a technique of teaching through debate still employed today, was founded by Socrates (hence the name) and described vicariously through Plato's writing. Students engage in dialogue with a "teacher," who facilitates learning by posing questions around a central issue and allows the students to arrive at the answers themselves through debate (although the answers are invariably the ones the teacher wishes, since students are led, through the debate, to accept the assumptions of the teacher's argument). Aristotle's ideas reigned unchallenged and unquestioned until the Enlightenment and Renaissance, and the value he placed on empirical observation led to the development of the scientific method, which is still taught in any science class today. English terminology such as logic, stoic, cynic, epicurean, or eclectic, though changed from the original meaning, reflects clearly the influence that Greek philosophy has had - more than two millennia later and on a completely different continent.

Greek philosophy provided many methods and techniques for logical argument. However, in Judaism, logic and debate were not overlooked either. The two prominent Jewish historians writing during the first century, Philo and Josephus, provide for us examples of Jewish debate and incorporation of Hellenistic ideas and philosophy. Philo, who lived from the time of Augustus into the reign of the emperor Nero, attempted in much of his writing to harmonize Greek philosophy and Judaism by means of allegory and symbolic interpretation. Philo was well versed in Greek literature, and employed allusions and references to epic poetry frequently. Using elements from Platonism, Stoicism, Pythagoreanism, and Aristotelian philosophy, Philo used his harmonization of philosophy as a means to defend and justify the Jewish faith. For example, by explaining the Creation in almost the same way as the origin of the universe is presented in Plato's *Timaeus*, Philo gives weight to Judaism for a Greek audience by tying the religion in with the ideas and "truths" presented by philosophers.

Our second historian, Josephus, discusses Philo in his *Antiquities of the Jews*, calling him, among a list of praises including his position as an ambassador and his eminence in all things, "one not unskillful in philosophy." This choice of praise clearly shows the high value placed on philosophy and being a philosopher. Josephus authored, along with a history of the Jewish-Roman war in which the Temple was destroyed (66-73), an *apologia* (a case and explanation) for Judaism. While more of a Romanized than a Hellenized Jew, Josephus records his argument for the significance of Judaism as a classical religion and philosophy in *The Antiquities of the Jews* and *Against Apion*. In this argument, Josephus outlines Jewish history from Creation, presenting Judaism as a religion that had existed even before the Greeks, and thus giving it classical authority (things that were ancient were considered to have weight and should be accorded their deserved reverence). He provides examples of the fathers of Judaism acting as ideal philosopher-leaders (an idea presented in Plato's *Republic*). Fathers such as Abraham, according to Josephus, taught science to the Egyptians, who in turn taught it to the Greeks. In doing so, he placed Greco-Roman culture and philosophy as owing a debt to Judaism. His and Philo's texts provide us with evidence that not only was debate and logical argument important to the Jewish culture in the first century, but that also great weight was given to the techniques of Greek philosophy (and also that information does not necessarily have to be historically accurate to carry weight and authority).

Having now outlined two other first century Jewish examples of the importance of reason and philosophical argumentation, I will now turn the analysis to Paul. As we discussed previously, Paul was born into a Hellenized Jewish culture. That is to say, much like Philo, Paul was born into an environment in which Jewish culture had been assimilated into Greek. Paul would then have been exposed to "the best of both worlds": Jewish and Greek education. We have explained the importance of logical argumentation and reason for two other Jewish writers of the day, but did Paul share the same sentiments? Paul may have called the "wisdom of the world" foolishness, saying, "Where is the wise man? Where is the scholar? Where is the philosopher of this age?" (I Corinthians 1:20), and declaring that he "did not come with eloquence or superior wisdom (I Corinthians 2:1)," nor claiming to give authority to his message "with wise and persuasive words (I Corinthians 2:4)," but that did not stop him from using logical argumentation when making his case to the Christians at Rome. Instead, Paul employs the basic tenets of logic to make his case: attempting to demonstrate the truth of an assertion (i.e. draw a conclusion) based on the truth of another set of assertions (i.e. premises).[17] In other words, Paul presents and supports series of premises, upon which he bases his ultimate conclusion, with the idea being that if the premises are true, and they lead to the conclusion, then the conclusion must be true (Socrates employed this method as well in his dialogues, as recorded by Plato).

As we have already discussed, Paul presents to the Roman Christians a case for Jesus being the completion of the Jewish covenant (the promise to Abraham) and the way to attain righteousness by faith. While the conclusion of this argument has already been addressed briefly, we will now examine a section of it in detail, in order to focus on the argument that Paul builds and the logical steps he employs to reach his conclusions. Paul first lays out the ultimate assertion or conclusion of his argument: "For in the gospel a righteousness from God is revealed, a righteousness that is by faith from first to last (Romans 1:17)." He continues by backing this statement with evidence from Habakkuk (in the Jewish Scriptures). Paul then turns his attention to mankind and how, despite the fact that "what may be known about God is plain to them, because God has made it plain to them...so that men are without excuse (Romans 1:19-20)," people decided to ignore God. The consequence of this ignoring being:

> They have become filled with every kind of wickedness, evil, greed and depravity. They are full of envy, murder, strife, deceit and malice. They are gossips, slanderers, God-haters, insolent, arrogant and boastful; they invent

ways of doing evil; they disobey their parents; they are senseless, faithless, heartless, ruthless. Although they know God's righteous decree that those who do such things deserve death, they not only continue to do these very things but also approve of those who practice them. (Romans 1:29-32).

Having first established the premise that God made himself very clear, so that there was no excuse (of ignorance, for example), and second the premise that mankind still chose to ignore God, resulting in the above description of the consequences, Paul then says, "You [Roman Christians], therefore, have no excuse (Romans 2:1)" for condemning others while doing the same actions. In other words, Paul uses the two previous premises to arrive at a minor conclusion: if there is no excuse for anyone, then there is no excuse for you. Paul then takes his discussion of "sin" toward judgment, stating the premise that "all who sin under the law will be judged by the law (Romans 2:12)." Even Gentiles who were not given the law but still obey its principles will be judged by it, "since they show that the requirements of the law are written on their hearts (Romans 2:15)." Thus, Paul illuminates the ultimate consequences for the earlier explained decision to ignore God.

Paul, having turned the direction of the argument toward the idea of being held accountable for actions under the law, then turns the focus of this premise to the Jews hearing this letter, asking them a series of hypothetical questions:

Now you, if you call yourself a Jew; if you rely on the law and brag about your relationship to God; if you know his will and approve of what is superior because you are instructed by the law; if you are convinced that you are a guide for the blind, a light for those who are in the dark, an instructor of the foolish, a teacher of infants, because you have in the law the embodiment of knowledge and truth -- you, then, who teach others, do you not teach yourself? You who preach against stealing, do you steal? You who say that people should not commit adultery, do you commit adultery? You who abhor idols, do you rob temples? You who brag about the law, do you dishonor God by breaking the law? (Romans 2:17-23)

In essence, by asking this series of hypotheticals (in not a dissimilar way to the Socratic Method) with the expected answers being "yes," Paul is providing an example of the premise he just finished discussing: had the Jews broken the law by which they would be judged?

Paul continues his discussion of Jewish law a bit longer, emphasizing the premise that circumcision (the mark that defined one as a Jew) meant nothing unless one observed the law, since circumcision was meant as a symbol of an inward "circumcision of the heart" (Romans 2:25-29). He then wraps up this part of his argument with the aptly phrased statement, "What shall we conclude then?" He then concludes that "Jews and Gentiles alike are all under sin (Romans 3:9)," supporting this statement with more evidence from Ecclesiastes, Isaiah, and multiple Psalms (Romans 9:10-18). Having laid out his premises, supported his argument, and drawn his conclusions, Paul then rephrases and condenses the argument again, thus drawing his final conclusions and laying the groundwork for the next section of his case:

Now we know that whatever the law says, it says to those who are under the law, so that every mouth may be silenced and the whole world held accountable to God (there is no excuse, and people under the law will be judged by the law). Therefore no one will be declared righteous in his sight by observing the law; rather, through the law we become conscious of sin. (Romans 3:19-20)

As analyzed earlier, Paul then uses his conclusion that no one can obtain righteousness through the law as a premise to explain that Abraham was declared righteous by faith, apart from the law, and that Jesus served as a way for this to be possible again. This short section illustrates the point very clearly that Paul not only employed, but valued logical reasoning, techniques and progression of argument when describing the earliest Christian theology.

Restored Logic and Reason

I would like to begin this section with a question: would the Truth be illogical?

In order to explore this question, I will need to go back to the statements of Paul about wisdom in I Corinthians. Paul asks the question, "Has not God made foolish the wisdom of the world (I Corinthians 1:20)?" He goes on to say, "When I came to you, brothers, I did not come with eloquence or superior wisdom as I proclaimed to you the testimony about God (I Corinthians 2:1)." On the surface of things, it appears that our arguments are contradicting Paul's statements in his letter to the Corinthian church. However, if you keep reading chapter 2, verse 6 takes a different turn: "We do, however, speak a message of wisdom among the mature, but not the wisdom of this age or of the rulers of this age, who are coming to nothing." So, Paul is making a distinction between the wisdom of the world and the message of wisdom "in words taught by the Spirit, expressing spiritual truths in spiritual words (I Corinthians 2:13)." When Paul calls the wisdom *of the world* foolishness, he refers to the philosophies themselves, those beliefs expounded by the Greek Philosophical schools of thought, examples of which have been described in the historical analysis, but not the methodology and techniques of logic used to present their arguments.

These beliefs, then, or "schools of thought" were the "wisdom of the world" to Paul. He correctly points out that the wisdom of the world was "coming to nothing." For Paul, it was foolishness to believe that nature and God were the same (Stoicism), that man could not understand Truth (Skepticism), or that God does not influence the world (Epicureanism). He does not say, however, that logical reasoning or thinking in progressive steps is foolish. He states clearly that he did indeed speak a message of wisdom, but not the world's wisdom. Instead, he spoke with the wisdom of the Spirit of God, attained from having the mind of Christ (I Corinthians 2:16). A cursory overview of the tenets of the Greek schools of philosophy reveals why Paul would call their *beliefs* "foolish," while presenting the Truth of Christ, taught by the Spirit, in a logical and stepwise manner, building argument upon argument to draw conclusions.

Paul's arguments employ sound logical techniques; yet, elements of the church today seem to have arrived at the conclusion that logic is "foolish," and that God's truth does not have to make sense. Some in the church seem to forget that Paul stated, "The man *without* the Spirit does not accept the things that come from the Spirit of God, for they are foolishness to him and he cannot understand them" (I Corinthians 2:14). Is Paul's assumption, then, that if I do have the Spirit of God, then I will understand the wisdom that comes from His Spirit? By rejecting logic, is the church admitting their lack of understanding of God's wisdom, thereby admitting to the absence of God's Spirit?

At the same time, many statements made in the current church contain logical fallacies. As such, it seems instead of honestly rejecting logic altogether, the church has used convenient logic, a progression of argument which is based in a false starting point or a false assumption which leads to a wrong conclusion, but which supports the point they are trying to make. Let me offer this example to illustrate my meaning: pretend that I was born and raised in a house with no windows or doors. Throughout my life, everyone I knew told me over and over again that the sky was green. Having never seen the sky, I took their word for it. One day, someone brought pictures of the outside in for me to see, and I noticed the large blue area on one side and the swath of green on the other. Logically, based on the false premise that I had been taught that the sky was green, I hang the picture on the wall green-side up. This decision puts the blue area on the bottom. My logic goes something like this: the sky is green (false premise); the sky is up; the grass is below the sky; the blue is below the sky; therefore, grass is blue (false conclusion). All my pictures end up hung upside down, because I have drawn a false conclusion based on a false premise. Later, I hear a song with the lyrics, "Blue skies smiling at me, Nothing but blue skies do I see." This chorus makes no sense to me, with my green sky schema, but wait, I can make it fit! The color blue is used to describe someone who is sad, as in "she has the blues today." So this song is actually talking about the singer being sad, thereby seeing "blue" skies, which are smiling a mocking smile. If you know this song, it is actually talking about good times, as in an unclouded day. As you can see, I have drawn another conclusion based on the original false premise, which is actually 180 degrees from the truth. In fact, it is a reality that the more conclusions I draw, and the longer I keep the false schema in place, the farther from the truth I will travel.

It is a basic tenet of logical argument that if you begin with a false premise, the conclusion must also be false. The same process of distancing from the truth occurs when I make a false leap in logic, assuming connections or cause-effect relationships where there are none. My original premise can be correct, but in one step I follow a false assumption to a false conclusion, and from there my entire premise is distorted, until it ultimately bears no resemblance to reality. In this case, the principle of logic states that if a different premise from the one stated can be proven true, then the conclusion must be false. For example, I could argue that when the cat is in the chair, the chair rocks (true premise). The chair is rocking (true premise); therefore, the cat must be in the chair (true or false?). To prove the logical fallacy, I would only need to point out that the chair also rocks when grandma is in the chair. This different premise is also true, and thus the conclusion made is false.

An instance of this kind of logical fallacy that you might have heard of follows: God's Word states that homosexuality is a sin; homosexuals live in New York; the 9/11 attacks on the World Trade Center occurred in New York; therefore, God must have been punishing homosexuals for their sin by the attacks. The leap of logic to this conclusion is not supported by this argument. To disprove the logic, I need only point out that homosexuals also live in Atlanta, San Francisco, St. Louis, Denver, and the list goes on and on. Therefore, the conclusion that God must have been punishing homosexuals with the World Trade Center attacks is false. A similar argument was espoused following Hurricane Katrina, which resulted in the conclusion that the decadence of New Orleans was the cause of God's punishment on the people of that city via the hurricane. In response, I would just like to mention that Las Vegas still stands and is thriving.

So let's apply some of these "rules" of logical argument to the four contradictory conclusions presented at the beginning of this chapter:

Argument #1: If the Lord's Prayer includes a request for God's will to be done on earth as it is in heaven, then God's will is not always done on earth as it is in heaven; therefore, some things that happen on earth are not God's will. The initial premise is true; the prayer recorded in Matthew includes those words. Is there another valid premise, other than the one suggested, that explains Jesus including these words in this prayer? Would Jesus, based on what is known of Him and His teachings, suggest praying for something that is already in place or has already been fulfilled? What about the rest of the requests in this prayer? Are any of those requests for things already fulfilled? Do we have a record in the Bible or elsewhere of any prayer of Jesus asking God the Father for things that had already happened? Do we have any other indications that Jesus would teach empty words that had no purpose to His disciples, for the sake of ritual or for show? If the answer to these questions is "no," and there are no other valid premises to explain the inclusion of those words, then the conclusion is true: if God's will is not always done on earth, then some things that happen on earth are not God's will. To make the assumption that, when something troubling or bad happens in my life, it is God's will for me, is a conclusion that cannot be drawn, based on the argument presented above.

Argument #2: Matthew 6:19-21 contains instructions for us about treasures on earth vs. treasures in heaven. This premise is true and accurate. The teaching states not to store up treasures on earth, but instead to store up treasures in heaven, for where your treasure is there your heart will be also. This is an accurate representation of the statements recorded in Matthew. Do we have any other indications of Jesus' views on riches? How about Matthew 19:21-23, which begins with Jesus saying, "If you want to be perfect, go sell your possessions and give to the poor, and you will have treasure in heaven." Is this statement consistent with the earlier Matthew verses? Luke 6:24 states, "But woe to you who are rich, for you have already received your comfort." Is this also consistent? What about the parable in Luke 12:13-21, which includes the statements, "a man's life does not consist in the abundance of his possessions" and "This is how it will be with anyone who stores up things for himself but is not rich toward God"? I could continue, but I believe the point is made. According to these verses, Jesus views earthly riches as a hindrance to storing up treasures in heaven, or being rich toward God; this would be a true premise based on these examples. Is it accurate to state the premise that Jesus would not desire to hinder us from being rich toward God or storing up treasures in heaven? Since a foundational belief in Christianity is that the cross of Christ made it possible for us to be saved, and that this was an act of purest love, it is a valid premise to assume Jesus would not want to hinder us but instead makes it possible for us to be rich toward God and to store up treasures in heaven. Therefore, given these valid premises, it is a valid conclusion that Jesus would not give us earthly riches as a "blessing."

Argument #3: It is a central tenet of Christianity that God loved us so much that He gave His Son to die on the cross, so that *whoever* believes in Him will not die but will have eternal life. Assuming that it is true that Paul is the earliest record we have of Christian beliefs and theology; does this statement match the gospel as recorded in Paul's letters and as described earlier in this book? Yes it does. Does this statement agree with the other writings of Paul in his undisputed letters? Let's see. There are numerous mentions of God's love expressed through Christ Jesus in Paul's letters. He describes in some detail Christ's obedience to death on the cross as an act of service and love. Without listing each one individually, this appears to be thematically true to Paul's writings. Therefore, if it is true that whoever believes in Jesus will have eternal life, then all who believe in Jesus will be saved. This is a true premise. How, then, did some Christians arrive at their belief that only those chosen and predestined by God would be saved? This appears to be a limitation on the reach of the saving power of belief in Christ. Would it be logically accurate to state: if all who believe in Jesus will be saved, then only those chosen and predestined to be saved will be saved. No, this statement is a logical fallacy. One cannot draw such a conclusion from the initial statement ('if all' means inclusive, 'then only' excluding cannot be true).

Go back for a moment to Argument #1: I have logically demonstrated the truth that God's will is not always done on earth as it is in heaven. However, Christians who ascribe to predestination would also most likely disagree with this conclusion. Why? The reason for both disagreements lies in one of their foundational stances, which states that because God is in control of every event, his will is always done; and therefore, man does not have free will, but rather, everything serves God's will. Let me state their arguments in the form of logic: If God is in control, God's will is always done. If God's will is always done, then man is subservient to God's will, negating his own free will. If man does not have free will, and God is in control, and some individuals are not saved, then it is God's will that some individuals are not saved. Therefore, God chooses those who will be saved and those who will not be saved.

Interestingly, it is in Paul's writings that these Christian groups claim support for their conclusions. The verses most commonly quoted are in Romans 8:

> And we know that in all things God works for the good of those who love Him, (alternate translations: And we know that all things work together for good to those who love God; or, works together with those who love Him to bring about what is good, with those) who have been called according to His purpose. For those God foreknew He also predestined to be conformed to the likeness of His Son, that He might be the firstborn among many brothers. And those He predestined, He also called; those He called He also justified; those He justified He also glorified. (Romans 8:28-30)

The focal words (foreknew, foreordained, predestined) used to support their premises have become "loaded," acquiring through years of theological debate many layers of presumption and assumption. So, in the spirit of the stated primary purpose of this book, I will attempt to go back to the original Greek words used by Paul to present an untarnished definition of the two words in question: foreknew and predestined. "Foreknew" is the translation given in NIV and NASB for the Greek word *proegno*. This word from two roots: *pro*, a primary preposition meaning before, and *gnosko* (like *gnosis*), a verb which means to know, to learn to know, come to know, perceive, feel, understand, become acquainted with, and interestingly enough, it is also a Jewish idiom for sexual intercourse (as in "he *knew* his wife"). Restated in the context, then, this word could be presented in English as, "for those God learned to know before," or "those God came to know before," or "those God perceived before," or "those God understood before," etc. It is also possible that, if put in English language order, the word could mean "before God knew," but this is very unlikely.

"Predestined" in the translation given in NIV and NASB for the Greek word *proorisen*, comes from two words as well: *pro* again, and *horiso*, a verb meaning to define, as in to mark out the boundaries and limits, or that which has been determined. Again presented in context, this word could then be restated as, "He also defined before," or "He also marked out the boundaries and limits before," or "He also had determined before." What was defined, marked out or determined before? That those who He had learned to know or come to know before would be conformed to the likeness of His Son. As you can see, this statement could very easily be understood to mean that God defined or determined beforehand that all those who He had come to know would be conformed to the likeness of Christ. In other words, it was the "conforming" that God predetermined or predestined, not the "who." Keeping in context, why had God predestined that those He had come to know would be conformed to the likeness of Christ? According to the text, it was so that Jesus would be the firstborn of many brothers, and those many brothers would also be called, justified and glorified, like Jesus. Remember that, earlier in chapter 8 of Romans, Paul had presented His argument that "what the law was powerless to do in that it was weakened by the sinful nature, God did by sending His own Son in the likeness of sinful man to be a sin offering. And so He condemned sin in sinful man (Romans 8:3)." Paul goes on to say that "if anyone does not have the Spirit of Christ, he does not belong to Christ. But if Christ is in you, your body is dead because of sin, yet your spirit is alive because of righteousness (Romans 8:9-10)." Notice the "anyone" as part of Paul's if/then premise presented in these verses. This premise is consistent with that of John

3:16, which states "whoever." Continuing his logical presentation, Paul states that those who are led by the Spirit are sons of God:

> For you did not receive a spirit that makes you a slave again to fear, but you received the Spirit of sonship… The Spirit Himself testifies with our spirit that we are God's children. Now if we are children, then we are heirs – heirs of God and co-heirs with Christ. (Romans 8:15, 16-17).

This entire logical argument immediately precedes the statements discussed above regarding what God predestined. As a continuation of the logical progression in the previous verses, it makes more sense that Paul was offering an expansion on or explanation of our position as children of God, and co-heirs with Christ, because God had determined beforehand that we who He knew (those who have the Spirit of Christ) would be conformed to the likeness of Christ. Otherwise, one could argue, how could we stand before God as a co-heir, if we were NOT conformed to the likeness of Christ?

So, using the rules of logic, I submit there is an alternative premise to the one proposing God chooses only some to be saved. The alternate premise I propose agrees with the premises that are foundational to the understood "gospel" of Christianity (John 3:16, Romans 8:9-10 and Paul's other descriptions of the "gospel"), while the "predestination" premise is contradictory to the foundational "gospel" of "whoever" and "anyone who" stated in the above parenthetical sources. Finally, I also submit that the argument of these groups of Christians begins with a false premise: that of man having no free will. I have presented in earlier chapters on Adam and Eve's choice, and in this chapter regarding the Lord's Prayer, a logical argument that shows that man does indeed have free will. Therefore, God does not pick and choose who will and will not be saved, for anyone who believes in Christ will be saved, and man has the choice to believe in Christ as Savior or to reject him (as supported by Paul's contrast in Romans 8 above between those with the Spirit of Christ in them and those who do not have His Spirit in them).

Argument #4: Paul's limited discussion on the activities of Jesus while alive has been presented in a previous chapter, but I want to revisit one of the aspects of Christ that Paul does discuss: that of His nature as a servant. Paul characterizes Jesus, on more than one occasion, as meek and humble, and specifically states in Philippians 2:5-7 that Jesus "made Himself nothing, taking the very nature of a servant." Yet, I have heard numerous sermons and read several Christian books that suggest Jesus demands our praise. Not simply that He has done praiseworthy things, which He certainly has and does, but that He expects our praise, even requires it. I have heard and read that before we can pray, we must offer praise, or our prayers will not be heard. This statement calls to mind an image of a haughty, arrogant, prideful and demanding God; a distant God Who folds his arms, snaps His fingers in expectation or taps His foot impatiently, turning His face from us until we "get it right." Once we have performed correctly (i.e., given the correct amount of praise), then and only then will He turn back and notice us, listen to us, and respond.

I have also heard and witnessed in action in so-called "contemporary" worship services, that "praise" must happen before we can be in the presence of God, and that through some magical formulaic ritual of standing up, lifting our arms in the air, singing fast songs to loud music and swaying with our eyes closed, we are "summoning" the Holy Spirit into our midst. (This is an example of a reductionistic understanding of reverence.) When we have done enough "praising," then the music softens, the singing slows, and we can begin to "worship" God, Who, ostensibly, has now shown up to receive our worship. Then we can pray (or give an introduction to the sermon from the stage with eyes closed while the music keeps playing softly in the background, and call it prayer). From the standpoint of a logical argument, does this premise make sense: Jesus, the meek and humble servant, the foot-washer in a towel, stands aloof and apart and unresponsive until we give Him His due in praise? As a Christian counselor studied in the more psychological understandings of self-esteem, I wonder if Jesus would really be that insecure, so uncertain of His own position as God, His own worth, that He would demand our acknowledgment before He would condescend to relate to us? I am unable to reconcile logically Christ the humble servant unto death on the cross with this prideful (yet insecure) view. In addition, I would point out that some of the very words I am employing to describe this view, Paul used to describe godless and wicked men, specifically "insolent, arrogant, and boastful (Romans 1:30)."

What, then, are the words about praising God, in Paul's letters and elsewhere, talking about? If you look in Paul's writing, his mention of praise of God was in response to something God had done, or to Who God was, rather than an attempt to elicit a response from God. For example, in the introduction to the letter known as II Corinthians (not Paul's second letter to this group, but the second letter that we have), Paul praises God:

> The Father of compassion and the God of all comfort
> (who He is), who comforts us in all our troubles (what

He does), so that we can comfort those in any trouble with the comfort we ourselves have received from God (our response to Him). (II Corinthians 1:3, parentheses added).

Similarly, in Romans 15:7-8, Paul states, "accept one another, then, just as Christ accepted you, in order to bring praise to God. For I tell you that Christ has become a servant of the Jews on behalf of God's truth, to confirm the promises made to the patriarchs." Christ accepts us; therefore, accept each other *in order to bring praise to God*. Paul seems to be describing something very different from God demanding His due. Instead, Paul presents God as receiving praise from our acceptance of others that began with His acceptance of us, and from our comforting of others that began with His comforting of us. In other words, God is praised through our natural response to His being a servant to us. If we truly know Who God is and we truly receive what He has done and does for us, then what we feel is humility (in other words, we receive His attitude of a servant), and what flows out of our hearts toward others is what God has poured into us, which then is received by God as praise.

Having addressed the four contradictions presented at the opening of this chapter, I would like to return now to the question that I posed first in Chapter 4: is there anything left that is beyond our understanding? To me this question is directly related to the one that opened this section of this chapter: would Truth be illogical? In other words, does God make sense? For, if God does not make sense and His Truth is illogical, then it is possible still, even with the revelation of Christ, that I could not understand it or ever grasp it, accommodate for it, or integrate it into my heart. This "wisdom" is the belief of the Skeptics, philosophers of ancient Greece. However, we already know Paul called that "wisdom" foolishness. But according to Paul, the wisdom of God, which he said was "Christ crucified: a stumbling block to Jews and foolishness to Gentiles (I Corinthians 1:23)," is revealed to us by His Spirit (I Corinthians 2:10). Christ, Paul said, is "the power of God and the wisdom of God (I Corinthians 1:24)," and "has become for us wisdom from God (I Corinthians 1:30)." Continuing his explanation of God's wisdom and God's truth, Paul states:

> We have not received the spirit of the world but the Spirit who is from God, *that we may understand* what God has freely given us. This is what we speak, not in words taught us by human wisdom but in words taught by the Spirit, *expressing spiritual truths* in spiritual words. (I Corinthians 2:12-13, italics added for emphasis).

So, God's wisdom and truth come to us from our reception of His Spirit, and through His Spirit we can understand them.

In the letter known as II Corinthians, Paul uses the story of Moses to illustrate how Christ has removed the veil over our hearts that kept us from seeing, and knowing, God:

> Now if the ministry that brought death, which was engraved in letter on stone, came with glory, so that the Israelites could not look steadily at the face of Moses because of its glory, fading though it was, will not the ministry of the Spirit be even more glorious?...Therefore, since we have such a hope, we are very bold. We are not like Moses, who would put a veil over his face to keep the Israelites from gazing at it while the radiance was fading away. But their minds were made dull, for to this day the same veil remains when the old covenant is read. It has not been removed, *because only in Christ is it taken*

Donna E. Lane, Ph.D. & Hayden J. Lane, M.A.

away. Even to this day, when Moses is read, a veil covers their hearts. But whenever anyone turns to the Lord, *the veil is taken away.* Now the Lord is the Spirit, and where the Spirit of the Lord is, there is freedom. And we, who with unveiled faces all reflect the Lord's glory, are being transformed into His likeness with ever-increasing glory, which comes from the Lord, who is the Spirit. (II Corinthians 3:7-8, 12-18)

Paul continues with this theme in II Corinthians 4:6: "For God, Who said, 'Let light shine out of darkness,' made His light shine in our hearts to give us *the light of knowledge of the glory of God in the face of Christ* (italics added for emphasis)." Because we can see and know Christ in our hearts, we can indeed know His truth.

Given this understanding, that we can know God's truth through Christ in our hearts, I would suggest to you that if some belief does not make sense; if it is contradictory to the character of God, or illogical in its formulation; and, if it brings with it anything that is not of God, such as confusion, despair, a heavy burden, shame or fear; then the belief must be false. There is no middle ground, no almost true or sort of true, in God's wisdom. Our understanding can be distorted, or the belief can be a counterfeit of God's truth, just slightly off True North on our compass but still eventually taking us to the South Pole (180 degrees from the truth); but in either case, it is still false and must be rejected. In response, instead of assimilating the belief into our existing schema, we need to set the belief in front of Jesus in our hearts and ask His Spirit to reveal the Truth to replace the false belief or our own understanding.

To illustrate the point I am making, I would like to share one of my experiences with the Lord where He created an accom-

94

modation in my heart for His truth. I had always believed Jesus was like a lighthouse on the shore, showing me the way to Him and guiding me through the storms of life. By the way, I had also read this analogy in a Christian book or two, so I know I was not alone in this belief. I accepted this belief rather matter-of-factly, like an "of course" that I did not question, a lovely little image to give me hope…or so I thought. One day, I was talking to Jesus and He brought this image back to my mind, including seeing myself struggling along in a tiny boat in the middle of a huge, dark storm, paddling literally to save my life while the boat I was in took on water with each wave. From the boat, I could see the distant light on the shore, and at the same time I began to hear an encouraging voice calling out to me: "You can do it! Keep bailing! Keep paddling!" So, sure enough, I paddled harder and I bailed furiously, but the water kept creeping up inside the little boat. It seemed nothing I could do would gain any ground on the raging storm and the rising water, and yet the voice on the shore kept calling, "Bail harder! Paddle faster! You can do it!" The burden of the struggle, which I had taken for granted and ignored previously, began to weigh heavily on me, enough so that I finally noticed it. But I was too afraid of losing sight of Jesus to take my eyes off that distant light. So I kept struggling, paddling, bailing…and losing. It was then that the true voice of Jesus spoke in my heart, and He said, "That is not me," referring to the "encourager" on the shore. He continued, "You have had your eyes on that 'light' on the shore for so long, and you have believed that was me for so long, that you never stopped to look beside you in the boat." At that point, exhausted from the struggle and willing to risk it because I was foundering anyway, I turned away from the distant light, and there was Jesus, sitting beside me in the boat, reaching His arms out to take me with Him. In an instant, I was inside a "lighthouse" with Jesus, His light shining all around me and shielding me from the storm. Only then could I truly understand how distorted my view had been. In fact, this distant, uninvolved perception of Jesus was completely contradictory to Jesus on the cross, the God Who took my sins onto Himself, one of the most hands-on, involved and loving actions one could imagine.

When examined logically in the light of Truth, the belief that I had thought brought me hope had left me alone, fearful and despairing. I was just so sure it was true that I didn't see it…until Jesus showed me His Truth. It was through this experience that Jesus first taught me about the deception of self-reliance. He is not the distant cheerleader who encourages us as we struggle, reinforcing our belief that it is up to us. He is the Savior Who takes us into His arms and brings us through the storm into His light. He is our Partner Who is with us in every moment, by our side in the storm *and* in the light, so that we are never alone. And He is the One Who establishes His Truth within our hearts as a shield and protection for us. He is the Kingdom of God within us.

Is this the Jesus you know?

Chapter 6

What is Faith?

The Current State of the Church and Faith

DURING A CONVERSATION WITH A FELLOW BELIEVER ABOUT faith, I was informed that the entire Christian church is suffering from a mass delusion. Of course, that is not what was meant, not overtly, but in reality that was what was said. In response to a question about the meaning of faith, this individual said, "For other people, it is 'I will believe it when I see it;' for Christians, it is 'I will see it because I believe it.'" I wanted to ask, "So, if I believe myself to have red hair, then when I look in the mirror I will see red hair?" In spite of the obviously ridiculous nature of my question (my hair is brown no matter what I wish it to be), this view seems to be widespread in the church. This statement was presented as one commonly accepted as true and oft repeated, almost like it was one of those rote messages we are all supposed to robotically speak when questioned on Christianity, our own personal Christian autoreply. Perhaps the individual was trying to talk about believing when you do not yet know, or perhaps he was suggesting that if I have enough faith of the right, adequate kind, then magical "blessings" will fall from the sky because I wish hard enough for it (recall the references to God as Santa Claus). Either way, I did not agree with his premise, and I was disconcerted that it was being so carelessly presented as absolute truth.

Faith today is seen as the prayer request insurance policy, my guarantee that I can manipulate God and control His response: "If you have enough faith then the Lord will do what you ask Him to do." Faith, or lack of it, is also the explanation for any problems that arise: "If you didn't get an answer to your prayer, then you didn't have enough faith." And faith in the church today is understood as acceptance or belief without knowledge: "When we don't know what is happening or why, we just have to have faith."

Something we don't do enough as a Body is to put ourselves in other people's shoes. For me, these statements, which I have heard on more than one occasion, are flagrant examples of our lack of empathy. Let's say there is a woman in your congregation who is a single mom, whose husband left her for another woman and skipped out on child support. This woman is barely making ends meet, working long hours and hardly seeing her children, who are developing behavior problems and acting out their anger at feeling neglected and unloved. Would you say this scenario is unheard of or even uncommon? I would say not. In a Sunday worship service, another woman is asked to give her testimony for what God has done for her in her life. She stands up and shares that God has brought her a loving Christian man to be her husband, something she has been praying for and has "believed God for," the current Christianese for having faith. Putting yourself in the first woman's shoes, what do you think her thoughts would be in response to that testimony? Would she wonder what she had done wrong, or how it was her fault that she was not similarly blessed? Would she assume she just didn't have enough faith? Would she therefore feel unworthy and condemned? How would you feel in her shoes?

How about another possible scenario: on any given Sunday there are any number of people in every church congregation who have sick family members; spouses, children, parents, etc. Every Sunday the church prays for those sick people and asks God for help and healing. Then one Sunday, someone gives testimony that God has healed his wife; that he prayed and all the family prayed and the church prayed, and because they put their faith in the power of God, God healed her. What would you then say to all those people dealing with illness in their family, those many, many people who had not been healed, if they asked why? Would you respond that God is random and capricious, or He simply doesn't care, or it is our fault for not believing strongly enough, or not saying the magic words, or not doing the right things? None of these thoughts are uplifting or encouraging. Yet, don't we get excited to hear some of these testimonies about "what God has done?" Unless, of course, we are one of the ones left feeling like an inadequate Christian, ashamed of and blamed for what has not happened in our lives.

Before I go any further, I want to clarify that I am not a deist, meaning I don't believe God created the world, then took off and left us to our own devices; far from it. It would be a typical evaluation to read the above examples, and in the usual human black-and-white thinking, come to the conclusion that since I am saying that it isn't true that He responds according to the measure of faith of the individual, then I am suggesting He isn't responsive at all. That is not what I am saying. I believe God is intimately involved with our lives, from the highly spiritual to the daily routine, from the crucial to the mundane. Instead, I am indicating that we do not control God. In other words, it is not in the power of the individual making the request of God to determine His response, based on our faith, or on any formula of any kind we might attempt to employ to elicit our desired response.

Is this another example of compartmentalization: we want to hear the good news and say thank you to God for it, but don't want to think about or look at the more difficult elements, for which we have no answer, because it messes up our comfortable belief set? Are we once again assimilating positive aspects into an existing schema, separating out the negative aspects that we don't know how to address under our existing schema, and refusing to deal with those things that do not fit? As I noted in Chapter 4, the response that "God is a mystery" seems to be followed immediately by either a change in subject or a lecture about "having faith." These two ideas seem to be closely linked, and both are certainly conversation stoppers. How can anyone effectively respond to either of these statements?

I believe the hurtful conclusions we draw that exclude a large number of individuals from His grace and love, like in the two examples offered above, grow out of distorted beliefs about faith in the church today. Faith is seen as more closely related to finger-crossing and defined more as wishful or even magical thinking (as in the conversation referenced above), and seen more as unquestioning acceptance, than as certainty from knowing God through relationship. So, if based on previous chapters, we can't resort to the "God is a mystery" argument, or the "it must be God's will" assumption, where do we turn for understanding of these questions?

Or is faith truly a means by which we manipulate God?

Historical Analysis

What does Paul have to say about faith, and how does he conceptualize faith? This is an extremely difficult question to answer, as Paul speaks of faith casually, in varied contexts, and with no real explanation or definition, assuming that his audience already knows what it is. In Romans, Paul uses the word translated as "faith" forty-eight times, the most of any of his letters. In the two letters we have to Corinth, the word occurs sixteen times: seven times in I Corinthians and nine in II Corinthians. Additionally, "faith" occurs twenty-seven times in Galatians, six times in Philippians, eight in I Thessalonians, and twice in Philemon, and this number is only a count of what has been translated into English as "faith." The same word that is translated as "faith" is also translated differently in other passages in correspondence to the contexts of the discussion. Having used the word over one hundred times in seven letters, and assuming that the churches knew what he meant, there must be some sort of definable concept of "faith" to the earliest Christians.

The Greek word translated as "faith," *pistis* (and its different forms), derives from the Greek *peitho*, "to persuade," and primarily means persuasion or conviction, or the grounds for having faith.[18] Paul employs the word in the context of persuasion through hearing in Romans 10:17: "Consequently, faith [*pistis*] comes from hearing the message, and the message is heard through the word of Christ." However, Paul uses *pistis* in a variety of different contexts, having multiple additional connotations besides persuasion and conviction, including trust (I Corinthians 2:5; "so that your faith [*pistis*] might not rest on men's wisdom, but on God's power"), trustworthiness (Romans 3:3; "Will their lack of faith [*apistia*] nullify God's faithfulness [*pistin*]?"), belief (Galatians 3:2; "Did you receive the Spirit by observing the law, or by believing [*pisteos*] what you heard?"), the contents of what is believed (Galatians 1:23; "'The man who formerly persecuted us is now preaching the faith [*pistin*] he once tried to destroy'"), unbelief (*apistia* in Romans 3:3 above), access to God's grace (Romans 5:2; "...we have gained access by faith [*pistei*] into this grace in which we now stand"), behavior expected from surrender to God (Romans 1:5; "...the obedience that comes through faith [*pisteos*]"), and degree of religious restriction (Romans 14:1-2; "Accept him whose faith [*pistei*] is weak...One man's faith [*pisteuei*] allows him to eat everything, but another man, who is weak [translated by the NIV as "whose faith is weak," which is implied but not said by the Greek], eats only vegetables").

Since the word means so much in so many contexts, it is difficult to provide a singular definition of what Paul meant by having faith. However, based on these contextual uses, it is possible to compile a composite "definition" of Paul's vision of faith. Faith begins for Paul with hearing his gospel and being persuaded. Not only does he state that, "faith comes from hearing the message (Romans 10:17)," but he makes all of his other conceptions of faith dependent upon hearing his gospel and being persuaded:

> "How, then, can they call on the one they have not believed in? And how can they believe in the one of whom they have not heard? And how can they hear without someone preaching to them (Romans 10:14)?"

Thus, to Paul, all of his other contextual ideas regarding faith hinge on first being persuaded by hearing his message. Working backward through this series of questions, after hearing the gospel and being persuaded by the message, people are to believe in (place their trust in) the one they heard about (through the gospel). Finally, they are to manifest this belief by calling on the one they believe in (the same one that they heard about).

Where then, do Paul's other contexts of faith fit in this model of hearing, persuasion, trust, and calling? Perhaps trying to find a singular definition is too narrow to represent the mental framework in which Paul employed *pistis*. Since Paul used the same word to imply so many different meanings, it also is possible that he saw little or no conceptual difference between persuasion, belief, trust, faithfulness, and the manifestations of these into practice. Analyzing the contexts in this way reveals that Paul would have viewed "faith" as a complex idea encompassing many different aspects. Is it possible that Paul perceived *pistis* in this way?

As an outside example of the same idea: that words can represent conceptual ideas rather than concrete definitions, I will employ another example of conceptual vocabulary. The Romans used a word, *res*, in an overabundance of contexts with just as many meanings. This word best translates as "thing" or "the things pertaining to..." Additional translations of this word are object, circumstance, case, matter, affair, business, transaction, fact, truth, reality, wealth, money, interest, politics, and history, as well as many more. To provide just a few examples of these multiple meanings, the *res publica*, translated as "Republic," literally means, "The things associated with the public." *Res divina*, "sacrifice," literally means, "The things that pertain to the divine." A philosopher named Lucretius authored a treatise entitled *De rerum natura*, which literally means "On the nature of things," but implies the concept of all aspects of the physical universe. Thus, through these brief examples, it becomes clear that other ancient people perceived words as relating concepts, and not just singular definitions.

As a modern example of this idea, consider the word "Love." Stop and think for a minute about the word, and try to give a concrete definition for it that encompasses all aspects of the concept. This is an incredibly difficult task, as the word represents a very complex conceptual framework and is employed to describe many different situations. Thus, the word "love" can be used abstractly to describe an indefinable warm, fuzzy feeling. One can "make love," representing a physical act. People are described as "falling in and out of love." "Love" can describe people's affinity for something, as in "I love pizza." There is a distinction between "love but not *in* love." Love denotes a set of behaviors evidencing the feeling, as you buy a ring to express your love. This example further illustrates the idea that certain words connote more than just a definition, but a complex and often abstract conceptualization of many different aspects to form an idea.

Therefore, since we have seen that not only in the time of the first Christians, but also today, people employ words that have more meaning behind them than a simple concrete definition is able to explain, it is perfectly reasonable to posit that Paul thought the same way. Because Paul used the same word to encompass a wide range of words all relating to a larger idea, his idea of "faith" can be extended to mean not just a single definition, but a conceptual idea encompassing all aspects of the contexts in which he uses the word. In short, in Paul's conceptual framework, "faith" means the entire model of being persuaded by hearing a message that inspires belief in and trust that God is trustworthy in his promise which results in calling out or surrender to God which obtains access to his grace and causes certain behaviors in varying degrees of strength or weakness based on the person's level of persuasion, belief, trust, and certainty in the ideas they heard.

Restored Faith

Even today, our concept of "faith" encompasses multiple meanings. I am going to focus on two of the main perceptions, and the ones that I think are most problematic: that faith is unquestioning acceptance without knowledge, and that faith is our way to manipulatively get what we want, through "prayer," based on our own efforts.

From the historical analysis, we can see that for Paul, the conceptualization of faith did not include any sense of an ability to manipulate God, or to receive "goodies" based on our amount of belief. Nowhere in his idea or presentation of faith exists the suggestion of manipulation, reward or deprivation, or wishful thinking. Paul mentions measure of faith in the context of using spiritual gifts according to the measure given to you by God (Romans 12:3-8), and strength or weakness of faith in the context of an instruction to not pass judgment over matters that are disputable because God accepts each person (Romans 14:1-4). Neither of these references indicates in any way that God is being controlled or manipulated in His response, nor is there any implication of more approval by God in either case. On the contrary, Paul makes God's full acceptance of each and every individual quite clear, "level" of faith notwithstanding.

In addition, the notion of faith in Paul's use of the word does not include the idea of faith as acceptance without knowledge. Instead, his definition includes the sense of firm persuasion or conviction. Certainty, surety, depth of acceptance, and even knowledge are all understood in the level of conviction portrayed in Paul's concept of faith. We can understand this because, as indicated in the linguistic review above, out of the persuasion through hearing comes trust, and trust comprises knowing, being certain through relational experiences, and being sure of something. For example, when describing Abraham's faith in God's promise that Abraham would be the "father of many nations," Paul describes Abraham as "being *fully persuaded* that God had power to do what He had promised" (Romans 4:21, italics added for emphasis).

Christians who argue that faith is believing while not knowing like to quote II Corinthians 5:7, which states, "We live by faith, not by sight." However, the context of this verse is in a discussion of being raised as Christ was raised from the dead (beginning in II Corinthians 4:14 and continuing through 5:9). This was something that Paul had seen for himself and was certain of, as he reported the appearances of Christ following His resurrection, and included, albeit last on the list, Jesus appearing to Paul (I Corinthians 15:3-7). Thus, Paul's discussion of living by faith was related to being still alive in our mortal bodies and therefore not at home with the Lord. He is saying that although we would prefer to be at home with the Lord, we continue to live, already knowing Jesus, and knowing that we will be raised as He was raised by God "so that which is mortal may be swallowed up by life" (II Corinthians 5:4). Paul's description of "not by sight" is, "so we fix our eyes not on what is seen (mortal life) but what is unseen (eternal life) (II Corinthians 4:18, parenthetical material added for clarification)." Paul even begins chapter 5 with the statement, "Now we know..." (II Corinthians 5:1, italics added for emphasis). So it is true that Paul had not yet seen his own eternal life when he wrote this letter to Corinth, but he *had* seen Jesus resurrected from the dead, and he had received "the Spirit as a deposit, *guaranteeing* what is to come (II Corinthians 5:5, italics added for emphasis)." For Paul, eternal life was not wishful thinking, it was guaranteed, and he knew and was certain of it.

However, inherent in Paul's conceptualization of faith is the inclusion of relationship. First I am persuaded by hearing the truth, and I trust God as trustworthy, making a "connection" with Him, and from that trust comes a calling out to God. These processes are internal in their nature, happening in my heart and mind in relation to God and with God. From that process flows out behaviors into my life. If faith has to do with relationship, with the elements of trusting and knowing God, such that knowing God is an understood feature of faith, then faith cannot mean belief without knowing.

Multiple times in his letters, Paul speaks of our justification by faith (Romans 1, 3, 4, 5, 9, and 10; Galatians 2 and 3); comparing the righteousness credited to Abraham because of his faith to the righteousness we receive through our faith in Jesus (Romans 4, Galatians 3). I would point out here that, according to the Old Testament story of Abraham, when his faith was credited to him as righteousness (Genesis 15:6), he already knew and had a relationship with God, a relationship that included a call from God, a promise and a covenant. Continuing in this vein, in Romans 10:8, Paul quotes Deuteronomy 30:14, "The word is near you; it is in your mouth and in your heart," and goes on to clarify, "that is, the word of faith we are proclaiming;" "for it is with your heart that you believe and are justified, and it is with your mouth that you confess and are saved (Romans 10:10)." In other words, faith (which justifies) is in our hearts, and calling on the Lord comes from our mouths, "for everyone who calls on the name of the Lord will be saved (Romans 10:13)." Recall our previous discussion on Romans 8, where Paul states that those who are led by the Spirit of God are God's children, and that we receive the Spirit of sonship, and not of fear. By that Spirit we cry, "*Abba*, Father (Romans 8:15)." Thus, it is understood in all of these writings that we know Jesus and receive His Spirit in our hearts as His children. This *is* faith, and through that Father-child relationship we are justified. It is then that we call on Him, as Father and Lord, and are saved. So I don't call out to an unknown entity, something wished-for but as yet alien to me; I call out to the God I know, His Spirit in my heart where the relationship is established.

In Romans 14:7-8, Paul states, "For none of us lives to himself alone and none of us dies to himself alone...whether we live or die, we belong to the Lord." What kind of relationship, then, is the relationship of faith? First, as indicated above, it is a relationship based on knowing. I know God, and He knows me. I suppose one could argue that I have a relationship of a sort with the grocery store clerk, in that I've met him and see him once or twice a week (sort of like many church-attending Christians). However, there is more to this relationship of faith.

Second, we know it is a relationship of love, as a good and loving father who would do anything, up to and including his own death, for his child's sake. God is a father who holds, shares with, cares for, and comforts his child every day, as a small child completely adores his or her father and feels totally safe with him. I guess that excludes the grocery clerk type of casual "relationship." Jesus is my best friend and He is more than my best friend. He is my partner, analogous to a good, strong, healthy marriage, but He is even more than that. He is also my Father and I am His child, with the fierceness of love that exists in a pure and untainted parent-child relationship. I specify here the type of parent-child relationship, because in my line of work I have the unhappy awareness of the painful nature of some parental relationships, which are contaminated by psychopathology, ignorance, or just plain selfishness. But with Jesus, there is no sin, no psychopathology, no lack of knowledge, and certainly no selfishness to infect and destroy that which is pure.

Third, we know it is a relationship based on trust. Trust means knowing what to expect, which comes as a result of individuals doing what they said they were going to do and being who they portray themselves to be. As Paul states, "What if some did not have faith? Will their lack of faith nullify God's faithfulness? Not at all! (Romans 3:3-4)." In other words, God is trustworthy in all and for all, and nothing about our faith or lack of faith can change that truth. In this element is another indication that the concept of faith as presented by Paul does not include any aspect of manipulation: God's trustworthiness is based on Who He is, not based on our response to Who He is. Is God, then, involved in our lives? Yes, intimately. Is this involvement based on our actions, behaviors, or beliefs? No, because God is Who He is, and His promises stand, and are not nullified, nor are they established, based on who we are or what we do. Our choice is to participate with Him as partner in His involvement, or to not acknowledge His involvement. He calls to us. Will we be persuaded and call out to Him? Whether we do or not, still He calls out to us.

Finally, we know it is a relationship of certainty, the certainty that comes from knowing God and experiencing God's trustworthiness. Not only in this relationship are we certain of God, it also allows us to be certain of His truth. As discussed more fully in Chapters 4 and 5, everything of God has been revealed to us in Christ; therefore, everything can be known and we can be certain of what has been revealed. So we know God, we know God loves us, we know what to expect from God, we are certain of Who God is and Who He says we are, and all of these together *are* faith.

This discussion might raise questions, then, about prayer. If prayer, as an action resulting from faith, is not intended as an avenue to manipulate or attempt to control God's response to us, then why pray at all? Like faith, prayer is about *relationship*. If you recall, Paul's cry to God of "*Abba*, Father" (Romans 8:15) is made as His child, heir and co-heir with Christ. Implicit in Paul's understanding of prayer, then, is a deep and intimate relationship. So, just as faith is our relationship with God, prayer is our interaction in that relationship.

Part of my private practice is marital and premarital counseling, and the vast majority of couples who come to my office for help report their primary difficulty as "communication." Thus, a major element of my job is to help them uncover the hindrances to communication in their marriage, and to assist them in deepening their intimacy through facilitating heart-level communication. Their problems do not lie in sorting out who will stop at the grocery store and what time dinner will be served. Where problems arise and develop is in the sharing of their hearts with each other: talking through their deepest feelings, risking complete vulnerability in opening up to disclose everything about themselves with each other, allowing their partner complete access to the hidden places in their hearts that no one sees and where no one goes. In a marriage, intimacy is developed through this type of heart-to-heart communication. The same is true of our relationship with God.

Just as I discussed regarding faith, nothing in this conceptualization of prayer points toward manipulation. Effective prayer does not mean overpowering God, it means *sharing* your heart and *listening* to God's response. Again, I want to emphasize that heart-level communication assumes a two-way conversation. The idea of prayer looking like begging and pleading with God to get a desired result, or bargaining with God to establish some kind of a quid pro quo deal, removes the quality of relational communication. I might beg and plead with a police officer to give me a break on a traffic violation, or make a list to give to Santa Claus of what I want in the way of presents in exchange for good behavior, but neither of these examples constitutes a loving, cherished relationship. I don't have an intimate connection with either figure, and this type of communication doesn't establish one. I'll either get the ticket or I won't; I'll either be excited on Christmas morning or disappointed. Nothing of ourselves is shared.

I indicated earlier in this chapter that I believe God is intimately involved with our lives, from the highly spiritual to the daily routine, and from the crucial to the mundane. It is through prayer, as defined above, that His involvement is evidenced. As I wake up in the morning, he is there and responsive to my greeting. As I make breakfast, he is sharing the experience with me, laughing at my inside jokes and silly comments back and forth with my son, Cody, enjoying with me my pleasure in the routines of the day. As I stood over Cody, lying in a hospital unable to breathe on his own, Jesus held me in His arms and spoke words of comfort to me, telling me about how He and Cody would one day play baseball together and I could sit in the stands and cheer them on…I could imagine no greater joy. As I sit at my computer and struggle to find the right words to convey what I am trying to describe about my relationship with Him, He suggests, "You could tell them about Cody." And so I will.

Chapter 7

Suffering

The Current State of the Church and Suffering

MY YOUNGEST SON, CODY, HAS A RARE, DEGENERATIVE AND progressive neurological disorder that he developed at 18 months of age. It has progressed in the last two years to the point where it is life threatening on a continuous basis. For example, he must have breathing assistance and oxygen at night to survive while he sleeps. He has been hospitalized four times in the last two years, intubated eleven times, and his heart has stopped twice. He is now 17 years old, and is one of those rare individuals whose presence immediately impacts those around him.

Because of his strong relationship with God, Cody has always believed that he could do whatever he set his heart and mind to do; in spite of what the doctors, the world, circumstances and appearances might have said to the contrary. What he has done is "impossible," according to everyone else but Jesus and Cody; and he has done more in 17 years than many people accomplish in a lifetime.

He has his second *dan* black belt in Tae Kwon Do, and he went for two consecutive years to the Junior Olympics in Tae

Kwon Do (in order to go you must finish in the top three in your state competition), where he received national recognition in the form of multiple medals for his indomitable spirit and perseverance. He played youth soccer, baseball, and football. He was the starting center on his football team, until he could no longer balance well enough to snap the ball, at which point, refusing to be deterred, he moved to tackle. His pediatric neuro-opthamologist stated it was impossible for him to read, with his uncontrolled jerky eye movements, yet he reads extensively, including such difficult works as the *Lord of the Rings* trilogy, and even the *Silmarillion* (a Tolkien history of middle earth, like reading a very long Chronicles in the Bible). In fact, he loves to read more than anything. The doctor said, flat out, it was a miracle. In spite of being told he would struggle with doing any schoolwork at all, academic testing shows him scoring up to Masters Degree level of comprehension in reading. Because he has difficulty with the fine motor skill of writing, he does all math, even complex problems, in his head. He is also quite a Bible scholar: our adult Sunday school leader has been emailing Cody for insights into Scripture.

In spite of his physical circumstances, he continues to have an unyielding positive spirit, smiling and joking virtually all the time (the nurses told us he was the very first patient they had ever had in the hospital ICU who smiled around an intubation tube), still saying he can do anything, never giving up or giving in. In the words of the ex-Special Forces trainer who serves as Cody's Tae Kwon Do Master, "There is something about Cody that reduces grown men to tears." His attitude, beliefs, and spirit cause even non-Christians to acknowledge that God has His hand on Cody. A handful of Cody's friends have made the observation that Cody has what they call "a direct line" to God.

A number of Christians, upon meeting Cody, have said to me, "God obviously gave Cody this illness to make him such a special person so he could impact others for Christ; it is all part of God's great plan." Some have observed, "Cody has been such a wonderful influence on your other two children. God probably gave Cody his illness so your other two children would not become prideful because they have been so especially gifted." Another favorite comment is, "Do you think God was trying to get your attention, to teach you something through Cody's illness?" To these, I respond, "So you are telling me that God would make my son sick on purpose? That God is such a poor teacher that the only way He can instruct us is to make someone we love suffer? That He would sacrifice my son toward some big agenda of His own? That my son's life is that unimportant, that insignificant to God?" Sometimes, I get a "yes," although sometimes something about my response elicits a change in language at least: "Oh, no. I simply mean God *allowed* Cody to get sick because He knew what great good would come from it for others." I reply, "So you are saying that I am a better parent than God our Father? If I could I would choose to take Cody's illness on myself a thousand times over rather than have him suffer through it. Do I love Cody more than God?" To me, "God caused" and "God allowed" are not really significantly different concepts. "So the example God wants us to follow as a parent is to step aside and allow it to happen if a rapist comes toward our daughter, because some good will certainly come out of that rape?" I query.

A few brave souls will continue in this conversation with me, trying to explain how much God loves Cody ("And in your opinion, this love is evidenced by causing him to suffer?" I often ask) or focusing on God being "in control," so I should trust that this is God's best for us and "have faith." Some quickly jump to some default position; such as the infamous, "there are just some mysteries of God that we will never understand." Most, however, simply walk away.

So you will not think that these types of responses are somehow unique to something about Cody's circumstances that I have not shared, or specific to my particular denomination or church only, I will tell you the story of another woman's child. I heard the story on Mother's Day at a church service, held in one of those "mega-churches," where it is like parking at the mall and literally thousands of people cram into two arenas to hear the preacher. This particular Sunday, the teaching portion of the service began with a video clip of the pastor interviewing a mother, in honor of Mother's Day, I assume. This woman's daughter had recently died in her early adult years of a brain tumor. Initially, the pastor and mother talked about the daughter, about her long-standing active presence in the church youth group, her belief in Jesus, and then about her struggle to get her mom to believe also. It was at this point that the pastor's questions turned toward the mother, who shared her history of alcoholism, and her belief, verbally supported by the pastor on the video, that God had killed her daughter to "get her attention" so she would finally stop drinking and become a Christian as her daughter had always wanted.

I have one more question in response: who in his or her right mind would trust someone who would do this?

Historical Analysis

Paul, when writing a letter to the church at Corinth, describes a personal problem that has plagued him with suffering:

To keep me from becoming conceited because of these surpassingly great revelations, there was given me a thorn in my flesh, a messenger of Satan, to torment me. Three times I pleaded with the Lord to take it away from me. But he said to me, 'My grace is sufficient for you, for my power is made perfect in weakness.' ...That is why, for Christ's sake, I delight in weaknesses, in insults, in hardships, in persecutions, in difficulties. For when I am weak, then I am strong. (II Corinthians 12:7-10)

Paul does not explain what this "thorn" is, but people have taken upon themselves to interpret it as any number of problems; from physical pain to spiritual temptation; from backache to homosexuality. Instead of attempting to extrapolate what exactly Paul suffered from, we will focus here on what examples he does list, why he lists them, what he defines as "suffering," and why he says suffering happens.

If he does not tell the Church at Corinth what his thorn was, what examples of suffering does Paul list instead? In the same letter to Corinth, Paul describes hardships he has endured:

I have worked much harder, been in prison more frequently, been flogged more severely, and been exposed to death again and again. Five times I received from the Jews the forty lashes minus one. Three times I was beaten with rods, once I was stoned, three times I was shipwrecked, I spent a night and a day in the open sea, I have been constantly on the move. I have been in danger from rivers, in danger from bandits, in danger from my own countrymen, in danger from the Gentiles; in danger in the city, in danger in the country; and in danger from false brothers. I have labored and toiled and often gone without sleep; I have known hunger and thirst and have often gone without food; I have been cold and naked. (II Corinthians 11:23-27)

In another letter to Corinth, he also explains, "To this very hour we go hungry and thirsty, we are in rags, we are brutally treated, we are homeless (I Corinthians 4:11)." Paul thus described suffering by lumping together natural hazards, hunger and thirst, and robbery, with imprisonment, corporal punishment, and persecutions from Jews, Gentiles, and even other "false brothers."

Many people have a false impression of the Roman Empire during the time of Jesus and the first Christians, due in large part to the church. I have heard it explained in churches how Romans actively and constantly sought after Christians and Jews to persecute and kill them, at all times. This is just not true. The Romans, by and large, allowed the Jews to retain their autonomy, provided they did not make trouble and paid their taxes. Thus, the Jews were fairly independent even under Rome's suzerainty, and were allowed to keep their own government structure, religion, and customs, as long as the leaders maintained order and paid Rome her dues.[19] Paul attests to this Roman attitude when writing to the church at Rome:

> Everyone must submit himself to the governing authorities, for there is no authority except that which God has established…This is also why you pay taxes… Give everyone what you owe him: if you owe taxes, pay taxes; if revenue, then revenue; if respect, then respect; if honor, then honor. (Romans 13:1, 6-7)

Thus Paul makes the clear assumption that respect for authorities (the Roman government) goes hand in hand with paying taxes. Two instances are often cited by churches as evidence for Jewish persecution: the first being the Jewish revolt in 66. However, it is important to realize that the Romans razed the Temple in Jerusalem as a *response* to the Jewish uprising. Roman armies did not go searching for Jewish towns to destroy for the sheer enjoyment of destruction, and Jewish and Roman relations were not always as strained as they were in the time leading up to the revolt. Until the Jews made trouble, the Romans more or less left them alone.

Churches also misrepresent the conduct of every Roman emperor based on a report that Gaius Caligula wanted the Jews to worship him, and commissioned a statue of himself to be placed in the Jewish Temple in 40. While Philo does report that Caligula viewed the Jews with suspicion because they did not worship him as a god, this does not mean that every Roman emperor wished to be worshipped. Instead, Augustus refuted his divinity multiple times, and Tiberius was largely unconcerned with his status in the emperor cult. Additionally, according to Josephus, Caligula was convinced by Agrippa to reverse the decision to erect his statue in the Temple, the statue was never built, and he never did anything to the Jews.

Throughout the majority of the first century, since Christianity was not separate from Judaism, Christians were simply part of a small, insignificant sect isolated in a corner of the empire, and largely ignored by Rome (like the Jews). It took a long time for Christianity to spread and diverge from its Jewish roots, and for Rome to take notice of the new "superstition." Thus, persecution of Christians by Rome was intermittent and regional at most until the third century, where we have evidence for the first systematic ban on Christianity. The examples that many churches use for persecution of Christians come from the second century, far removed from the generation of Paul. The only description we have of a time when Paul was alive comes from the historian Tacitus, writing in the second century and describing Nero. According to Tacitus, Nero blamed a gigantic fire that swept through Rome in 64 on the Christians, instituting a persecution of Christians at Rome that died when he did in 68. Tacitus also reports the attitude (at least the attitude of the second century projected backwards) towards Christianity as a harmful superstition, *nova et prava* (new and depraved), that undermines Roman values and Christians as people who hate mankind.[20] As we have already analyzed, the Romans shared the belief that the more ancient something was, the more true it was, the more authority it had, and the more reverence it deserved. Thus, Josephus would argue that the Jewish religion deserved respect because it was older even than that of the Greeks. This is just one of many possible explanations for why the Romans would view Christianity as a harmful superstition: because it was new.

Other than this account by Tacitus, the author Lucian, writing in the mid second century, describes in his satire *The Death of Peregrinus* how Christians are gullible and overly generous. In his satire *Alexander the False Prophet*, Lucian associates Christians with atheists and says that people were ordered to drive them out of town. Pliny the Younger, in a letter to the Emperor Trajan from the early second century, explains that Christians are harmless, but that he imprisons and kills them because they are stubborn. Trajan replies that Christians were not to be sought out, but only punished if brought before a magistrate by a reputable means of accusation (no anonymous charges were permitted), and only after they were given the opportunity to recant. These letters present a rather loose policy toward Christians: that Pliny would not know how to handle them and that Trajan would reply, in essence, that he was to ignore them unless charges were actively brought.[21] However, it is a common misperception today to lump centuries of time together and treat these few and late reports as if they represent every Roman emperor and the entire history of Roman relations with Judaism and Christianity, such that *Jesus* was even born into a world where *Christians* were actively, methodically, and ruthlessly persecuted by an emperor who thought himself a god on earth and killed anyone who would not worship him (If you missed the irony of this statement, look again at the italicized words).

What then, were the "persecutions" that Paul and the early Christians endured? Through Paul's description, it seems as though the majority of his troubles came from Jewish authorities. Paul states that he received, from the Jewish authorities, thirty-nine lashes on five occasions. He then immediately discusses three incidences of being beaten with rods, followed by a stoning. He does not overtly state who inflicted these last two punishments. However, stoning was a particularly Jewish method of punishment, especially in religious matters of blasphemy and apostasy. This is only speculation, but by sandwiching the beatings with rods between the overt statement that he received lashings from the Jewish leaders and his stoning (understood as a Jewish punishment for religious offences), Paul could be implying that he received the beatings from Jewish authorities as well. However, even if Roman authorities beat Paul with rods, it was still less punishment than he had received from Jewish leaders.

Since, as we have already noted, Christianity began as a sect of Judaism, then early Jewish persecutions of Christians can be more correctly seen as Jewish internal sectarian struggles. There are many possible reasons why Jews would persecute those of their own who followed Christ's teachings. That Paul was stoned implies that he was accused of blasphemy or renunciation of God's law (which could fit with interpretations of some of the teaching found in his letters). However, this is not what we are analyzing. Suffice it to say that Paul received most of his trouble from the group to which he used to belong when he himself used to persecute the Jewish followers of Christ (I Corinthians 15:9, Galatians 1:13, Philippians 3:5-6).

In addition to lashes, beatings, and a stoning from the Jewish authorities, Paul also claims persecution from Gentiles, which more than likely resulted in his incarcerations. Paul could possibly have been viewed as a troublemaker by Roman authorities, especially if he was preaching about God coming to establish a kingdom (which may have been seen as sedition). Thus he might have attracted their attention and warranted his imprisonments since, as we have discussed, Romans only bothered with people who threatened to disrupt order. Paul finally says that he had been persecuted by "false brothers," presumably those he mentions in Galatians, which we have examined earlier. Paul has more to say about these persecutions, and how they took the form of slander: "[S]ome say, 'His letters are weighty and forceful, but in person he is unimpressive and his speaking amounts to nothing' (II Corinthians 10:10)." Persecutions are not the only sufferings that Paul mentions. He also includes in his list many hazards that accompanied his lifestyle of constant travel: shipwrecks, dangerous river crossings, bandits, hunger and thirst, being cold, and losing sleep.

Returning now to Paul's description of his "thorn," how would he have viewed this problem in light of what we have previously examined? He states that he was afflicted to keep him from becoming conceited, because of the revelations he received from God. If he received the revelations from God, did Paul's theology hold that he received the "thorn" from God as well, in order to keep him humble? If Paul did indeed believe that God caused him to suffer to keep him in his place, then why does he immediately associate the "thorn" with an agent of

Satan? This opinion: that Satan, or one of his agents, causes suffering, is also evidenced in other parts of Paul's letters:

> When we were with you, we kept telling you that we would be persecuted. And it turned out that way, as you well know. For this reason, when I could stand it no longer, I sent [Timothy] to find out about your faith. I was afraid that in some way the tempter might have tempted you and our efforts might have been useless. (I Thessalonians 3:4-5)

Paul even discusses the "false brothers," those who had been persecuting him through slander, in the same light:

> For such men are false apostles, deceitful workmen, masquerading as apostles of Christ. And no wonder, for Satan himself masquerades as an angel of light. It is not surprising, then, if his servants masquerade as servants of righteousness. (II Corinthians 11:13-15)

Paul also explains his traveling hardships as Satan's influence:

> ...out of our intense longing we made every effort to see you. For we wanted to come to you – certainly I, Paul, did, again and again – but Satan stopped us. (I Thessalonians 2:17-18)

In order to fully appreciate these statements, we must understand that Paul saw the world as being filled with supernatural forces. A war was waging all around Paul, in which many different angels and benevolent servants of God (including Paul and the other Christians - see II Corinthians 10:3) fought against just as many evil demons and servants of Satan. Even the Greco-Roman gods, in Paul's view, existed, but were demons.

He explains, "indeed there are many 'gods' (I Corinthians 8:5)," but he also states that "the sacrifices of pagans are offered to demons, not to God (I Corinthians 10:20)." Paul even viewed "sin" as a supernatural force, rather than a state of being. In other words, people are "under sin" in the sense that the force of sin holds sway over their lives. Looking back at the passage from I Thessalonians, then, Paul makes the clear link between persecutions of the church and the "tempter," a supernatural force that could have destroyed their faith.

If Paul makes the association between suffering and malevolent supernatural forces, then what was God's role in sufferings and humanity? According to his letters, God comforts and gives power to Paul, the apostles, and those suffering in the ancient churches. Thus, Paul understands that Christ's "power is made perfect in weakness." Lest this appear to be a singular occasion, or that Paul is only discussing an answer to a prayer that he alone received, we will look at other examples where Paul argues the same point: that God comforts, gives power, and delivers people from suffering:

> "But we have this treasure (the light of the knowledge of the glory of God that shines in our hearts - II Corinthians 4:6) in jars of clay to show that this all-surpassing power is from God and not from us. We are hard pressed on every side, but not crushed; perplexed, but not in despair; persecuted, but not abandoned; struck down, but not destroyed. (II Corinthians 4:7-9)

And again:

> Praise be to the God and Father of our Lord Jesus Christ, the Father of compassion and the God of all comfort, who comforts us in all our troubles...For just as the sufferings of Christ flow into our lives, so also

through Christ our comfort overflows…And our hope for you is firm, because we know that just as you share in our sufferings, so also you share in our comfort (II Corinthians 1:3-7)

Furthermore:

We do not want you to be uninformed…about the hardships we suffered in the province of Asia. We were under great pressure, far beyond our ability to endure, so that we despaired even of life. Indeed, in our hearts we felt the sentence of death. But this happened that we might not rely on ourselves but on God…He has delivered us from such a deadly peril, and he will deliver us. On him we have set our hope that he will continue to deliver us. (II Corinthians 1:8-10)

Finally, having analyzed what sufferings Paul endured, how he saw suffering as being caused, and what role God played in suffering, we must understand why Paul "delights" in suffering. This joy in affliction stems from two beliefs: that he is imitating Christ in suffering; and that it is not the physical circumstances, but the spiritual, which are important. Thus Paul can declare, "…as servants of God we commend ourselves in every way: in great endurance; in troubles, hardships and distresses; in beatings, imprisonments and riots; in hard work, sleepless nights and hunger… (II Corinthians 6:4-5)." Paul explains these beliefs for the church in Corinth:

Therefore we do not lose heart. Though outwardly we are wasting away, yet inwardly we are being renewed day by day. For our light and momentary troubles are achieving for us an eternal glory that far outweighs them all. (II Corinthians 4:16-17)

Additionally, Paul exhibits both of these beliefs when addressing the church at Rome:

> Now if we are children, then we are heirs – heirs of God and co-heirs with Christ, if indeed we share in his sufferings in order that we may also share in his glory. I consider that our present sufferings are not worth comparing with the glory that will be revealed in us. (Romans 8:17-18)

Restored Understanding of Suffering

How does Cody perceive his "suffering"? I put the word "suffering" in quotes because I know he does not see it as suffering at all. But why doesn't he see it as suffering? Anyone from an outside perspective would definitely call it suffering. He is a 17 year old who can never be alone and can never be away from his parents. That, in and of itself, would make most teenagers fall into the deepest depression, and even hopelessness. He can't go "hang out" with his friends; he can't go out to school even though he is incredibly intelligent, because of his physical needs; he has to wear machines to sleep and deals with constant alarms going off all night; he faces his own mortality as a present reality on a daily basis...just to name a few issues he deals with. But he still doesn't consider himself as suffering.

The other day, Cody and I were talking with a young man, the son of a friend of mine, who was feeling quite put out by his circumstances and who had decided selfishness and out-of-control behavior would make him feel better somehow. I suggested instead that he consent to literally put himself into Cody's shoes for a week, to which he initially agreed. However, when Cody began asking him how he would handle some of the issues Cody handles on a daily basis, the young man said, "If I had to do that for a week, I would kill myself!" I asked him if he believed Cody was depressed or "suicidal" and he responded, no, of course not (Cody has a constant smile on his face, ranging from a grin to a beaming glow). Suddenly, the young man's eyes began to widen, as if a light bulb had gone off in his head, and he stated, amazed, what was obvious to me: "Cody is not struggling with all this." The contrast of his own superficial circumstances, that he thought were so intolerable, with Cody's obvious difficulties, along with the disparity between his own selfish attitude and Cody's positive one, became apparent to him for the first time. However, he was not able to see or express what it is Cody has or what Cody knows that alters the apparent struggle into great joy and peace. I would venture to say that, if asked the same questions, most Christians would not really understand it or be able to explain it either.

Before I can effectively present the truth of what Cody has and what he knows, I will need to address the misperceptions and misrepresentations of the church. The first misperception is seeing God as the One Who either causes or prevents the suffering. Looking first at prevention, let's revisit Adam and Eve (Genesis 3). If God was going to "prevent" suffering, which includes the consequences of sin in the world and in the choices of each individual, and the deceptions of the enemy, would He not have chosen to prevent the introduction of sin into the world in the first place? Would He not have prevented Eve and subsequently Adam from either hearing or responding to the enemy's lie? Instead, according to the story, God speaks the truth to Adam and Eve, He warns them of the consequences of their choices, and He allows them the freedom to choose. This same pattern continues throughout the Old Testament. Other examples of this free will process have been described in previous chapters, so I would like to move forward to God's actual response to suffering: redemption.

The most obvious example of God's redemption is found in the very "gospel" as described by Paul. On the cross, Christ *redeemed* all humanity from the consequences of sin (eternal separation from God) by becoming a sin offering for us: "God made Him who had no sin to be sin for us, so that in Him we might become the righteousness of God (II Corinthians 5:21)." Another way of saying this truth is that Jesus took on our suffering (the consequences of sin) so we wouldn't have to suffer. If this desire of Christ to remove our suffering were not the case, why would He take on the cross? Why be born at all? Why put Himself into frail and completely human hands as an infant? Surely there were other options! Some kind of miraculous, turn-back-time transformation of the world back into Eden, or simply cutting to the chase and destroying evil and death with a dismissive wave of His hand, comes to mind. Why would He, "Who, being in very nature God, ...not consider equality with God something to be grasped, but made Himself nothing, taking the very nature of a servant, being made in human likeness. And being found in appearance as a man, He humbled Himself and became obedient to death – even death on a cross (Philippians 2:6-8)!"? *The cross itself demonstrates that He does not cause our suffering; He redeems it!*

What, then, causes our suffering? As indicated above, there are three sources of suffering in this world, each interacting with the other: the presence of sin, which came into the world through Adam (Romans 5:12-14); the choices of individuals, both my choices and the choices of others; and the deceptions and actions of the enemy. The presence of sin brings with it such things as disease and death, grief and loss, hard labor and pain, and hunger and thirst. The actions of the enemy include deception, distortion, and counterfeit promises designed to solicit our cooperation in his plans against God, which always involve our destruction. The enemy's plans are subtle and he is skilled at deceiving. Therefore, we usually don't see the outcome as our own destruction until it is upon us, or we feel too far-gone to be redeemed. The enemy, who doesn't care one iota about what happens to us, knows this hurts God because of God's great love for us, and that is the purpose behind his plans. Satan is the game player, the one who manipulates our lives toward his ends; not God.

Then, each one of our choices has consequences, whether positive or negative. The choices we make based on sinful desires, selfishness, fear, and agreement with evil carry with them negative consequences. Our choices also inflict consequences on others. If you don't believe this is the case, let me ask you if you have ever paid a deposit for an apartment or utilities? Do you know why you must pay that deposit? The answer is the failure of others to pay their bills, or their choice to destroy property and not make amends for the damages. Even if you have always paid your bills on time, or have never damaged property belonging to another, you will still be required to pay the consequences for the actions of others. This simplistic example is to make the point; there are horrible examples of the consequences of the choices of others that we could explore, such as murder, rape, child abuse…the list seems endless. However, I would like to refer back to Cody's story to present a very personal example.

Cody was not born with his neurological disorder. During his infancy, my family was invited to join another couple on a vacation trip to Hilton Head, SC. We were to meet the other couple at a condominium and spend a few relaxing days enjoying the sun and ocean. Prior to leaving, the couple called us and informed us that the man had been sick while on the trip, but his doctor "assured" him it was not contagious, so it was safe to come on down. At this point, I did receive a warning in my spirit from the Lord not to go. However, I was concerned with hurting the couple's feelings by backing out, so I ignored the warning and we went. When we returned home, Cody became extremely ill, and within a short time began to develop hand tremors and opsoclonus, which is spasmodic jerking of his eyes. Our pediatrician, terribly concerned, sent us immediately to the hospital, where a complete battery of tests was performed. The doctors found damage to the myelin sheath in Cody's cerebellum, which the neurologist attributed to an overreaction of Cody's immune system during extreme pressure of dealing with the initial illness. Some time later, we discovered that the doctor who was treating the man actually did tell the couple that his disease was contagious and he should not be around children. The couple chose to lie. Cody has been living with the consequences of that lie since that time.

True to His nature as described in the stories of the Old Testament, God warned us of the consequences of our actions, but He did not prevent our going on the trip. What He has done is to redeem, beautifully and completely, the consequences of that lie. Cody has the type of intimate and deep relationship with Jesus that wise men, theologians, and monks seek their entire lives, and very few individuals ever find. Of all the people I have met in my lifetime, Cody is the one I would say truly lives "the kingdom of God is within."

Do I believe that God caused, or allowed, Cody's illness in order that He might develop that type of relationship with Him? My answer is, absolutely and positively, no. The lie caused Cody's illness. I am certain that Jesus loves Cody with an even greater depth of feeling than Cody has for Jesus. I am also completely sure that Jesus weeps over Cody's bodily struggles, and that Cody developing this illness was not His will. Finally, I am comforted that He has redeemed all in response to the actions of evil on the part of the other people involved, rendering evil powerless in Cody's reality.

Some might claim that since God did not stop us from going, then He "allowed" this course of events to happen. I have two responses to that assertion: first, my view of "allowed" is, as I have alluded to earlier, a father stepping aside to move out of the doorway to let a rapist have at his daughter. God did not do that to Cody; in fact, He did attempt to stop us from going, by warning us of trouble. This statement leads me to my second response: God, having chosen to give us free will at the creation of all mankind, continues to interact and operate with us accordingly. In other words, God did not remove the free will choice of the couple to lie, nor did He remove our free will choice to go on the trip, even though both actions were for the wrong reasons. This is an important question, and we will deal in depth with the subject of control vs. choice in the next chapter.

The second misperception of the church that I want to address is the idea that God brings suffering to teach us lessons we need to learn, as if suffering is a form of discipline from God. I will begin by pointing out that Paul, in his undisputed letters, mentions discipline from God only once. This reference is found in I Corinthians 11:17-34, in the context of the harmful practices occurring during the "Lord's Supper" at the church in Corinth. As Paul describes it, he makes clear that "it is not the Lord's Supper you eat (v. 20)," because they behave without thought or consideration for others, some eating and drinking all available while others go hungry. Paul reminds the church of Jesus' words on the night He was betrayed, and concludes, "whenever you eat this bread and drink this cup, you proclaim the Lord's death until He comes. Therefore, whoever eats the bread or drinks the cup of the Lord in an unworthy manner will be guilty of sinning against the body and blood of the Lord (I Corinthians 11:26-27). " Paul instructs the readers of his letter to examine themselves before participating, "For anyone who eats and drinks without recognizing the body of the Lord eats and drinks judgment on himself (v. 29)." In other words, if you eat and drink for the sustenance of food and for drunkenness instead of out of belief in the saving power of Christ, you are still under the judgment of the law, and your sins will be judged accordingly. In fact, Paul concludes, "That is why many among you are weak and sick, and a number of you have fallen asleep (I Corinthians 11:30)." These are the consequences of sin, as I indicated above: our own destruction. Paul then makes an extremely interesting statement: "But if we judged ourselves, we would not come under judgment (v. 31)." In the context of all of Paul's extensive teaching about our inability to follow the law and therefore avert judgment according to the law, what does he mean here? Paul is indicating that, if we were capable of truly "judging" ourselves, if we were able to see our sin and as a result choose to follow the law instead, we would not come under the judgment of the law. However, we are not. We cannot save ourselves. Without "the body and blood of Christ," we would all be condemned; this is clear in Paul's "gospel." So, Paul continues, "When we are judged by the Lord, we are being *disciplined* so that we will not be condemned with the world (v. 32, italics added for emphasis)." Here is Paul's sole mention of discipline from God, describing His discipline as the consequences of judgment for sin that *they had chosen* based on their own refusal to believe in His salvation and God's offer of grace, "so that we will not be condemned with the world."

At this point, it would be beneficial to understand the meaning of the word, "discipline." The Greek word used here (*paideuometha*) is defined: "to train children, to be instructed or taught or to learn, to cause one to learn." The noun form of "discipline" is "disciple," which is someone who sits under teaching to learn. However, the word today has taken on a different meaning: that of punishment. The church today has actually provided us with a word that more accurately represents the original connotation of "discipline" by verbing the noun form. As a result, there are "disciple leaders" who "disciple" people who are new to the church or the faith. Substituting "discipline" for "disciple" in the above phrase does not make sense, because the meaning of "discipline" has changed. However, if you substitute "instructed" or "taught," or even "discipled," for "disciplined" in the above verse: "When we are judged by the Lord, we are being instructed, taught, or discipled so that we will not be condemned with the world;" it removes any connotation we have from our own use of the word "discipline" as interchangeable with "punishment." To be instructed and taught as a child does not carry a punitive meaning and no suffering is understood as a given part of that process.

In the above section of this letter to Corinth, Paul is instructing the disciples of that church how to behave in regards to the Lord's Supper. Specifically, he is dealing with a problem of selfishness that had been occurring at the table by teaching them to come with the right motivations, and to demonstrate their understanding of the Lord's Supper by eating at home, if they had food to eat, in order that others who did not have adequate food would be fed and cared for by the group. At the same time, Paul is describing the Lord's discipline as the consequences of sin and His action to save us from sin. As Paul described in Romans 7:

> For when we were controlled by the sinful nature, the
> sinful passions aroused by the law were at work in our

bodies, so that we bore fruit for death. But now, dying to what once bound us, we have been released from the law so that we serve in the new way of the Spirit…I would not have known what sin was except through the Law…But in order that sin might be recognized as sin, it produced death in me through what was good (the law)…Who will rescue me from this body of death? Thanks be to God – through Jesus Christ our Lord! (Romans 7:5,7, 13, 24-25, parenthetical content added for clarity).

God's discipline, then, takes the form of consequences and redemption. Consequences are the natural "fruit" or results of our choices; redemption rescues us out from under those consequences. Therefore, God's discipline does not take the form of suffering, beyond what occurs as a natural result of our own choices. He does not inflict suffering on us to teach us a lesson. Instead, we inflict the suffering on ourselves, as Paul is describing in his Corinthian letter. God then redeems our bad choices. "And we know in all things God works for the good of those who love Him… (or *And we know that all things work together for good to those who love God*, or *works together with those who love Him to bring about what is good*) (Romans 8:28)."

A third misconception of the church is that God does not value our physical bodies, or the physical realm for that matter, and therefore, to save our spirits He will inflict pain and suffering on our physical bodies. For this belief, I want to refer back to the mother who believed her daughter had been killed to "get her attention" so she would be saved. In her belief, and the belief of her pastor, since her daughter was already saved, her physical body no longer mattered, and the mother's salvation was the only issue at hand. The grief and suffering brought about by both the tumor and the girl's death were irrelevant.

They brought the mother to Christ, so that is all that mattered. Why, then, did Paul write, "For to me, to live is Christ and to die is gain. *If I am to go on living in the body, this will mean fruitful labor for me* (Philippians 1:21-22, italics added for emphasis)." Here, Paul speaks of the value of continuing to live, which *is* Christ, even though for Paul, and for each of us who are saved, departing from the body is "better by far" (v. 23). I wonder, though, if it is true that there is no value in our physical existence, then why doesn't our physical body simply evaporate or become dust the instant we receive Him as our Savior? Surely, if every new Christian were immediately transformed into spirit as he or she prayed to receive Christ, this would get the attention of the unsaved much more effectively than watching us live out our lives constantly falling short of the glory of God. How many unbelievers do you know who claim the hypocrisy of Christians as a primary reason for their refusal to consider belief in Christ? Yet, we do not disappear physically and rise mystically from the altar when we receive salvation. Could this be because Christ also values our lives? According to Paul, the answer is yes, for "to live is Christ."

I would like to explore Paul's statement further, beginning by pointing out that Paul did not say, "to live is worthless" or "to live is meaningless," before he went on the say, "to die is gain." He could have said either of those phrases, but he didn't. As I ponder his choice of words, "to live is Christ," I am aware that some might try to see the phrase as indicating some task or chore we must complete, assigned by Christ, before we can move on to the second phrase in the sentence, "to die is gain." Those individuals might agree that our lives have value, but they would say the value is in our "assignments," what we *do* for Jesus. In the case of the daughter with the brain tumor, these interpreters would view her "task" as converting her mom, which she accomplished by dying. I believe, however, that if these individuals knew the part of the story where the mother fell into a deep depression after her daughter's death, even attempting suicide before finally being hospitalized months after her daughter had gone home, they might pause and reexamine their interpretation. My observation is that, if this was an intervention by God to bring this woman into His "loving" arms (I put this in quotes not to indicate God isn't loving, but to suggest that this particular view of God is anything but loving), it was an extraordinarily inefficient one. Not only was it inefficient, but it could have just as easily resulted in the mother's death by suicide before she accepted Christ, or the imbedding of a deep anger and hatred toward God that the woman would have struggled to relinquish. If not in this case, these types of responses have happened in countless other cases where children have died, and the parents could not bear to continue to live, or raged at God for the remainder of their lives. Broken marriages, suicide, debilitating depression, developing alcoholism or another addiction, and rejection of God because they do not understand "why He took" their child, are actually the most common responses. How do you explain those cases, if in those cases, the child's death was caused by God to "get their attention"?

Recalling that we have argued that God's actions will make sense and can be understood, I now point out that the "logic" of this interpretation falls apart under the most superficial examination; therefore, logically, another explanation will exist. I suggest that the view of God as the Redeemer, rather than the Killer, makes sense, is consistent with the character of God presented in Scripture, and stands up to examination. As I indicated earlier in this chapter, God's redemption of Cody's illness has removed the power of the original lie, and Cody continues to reap the benefits of God's redemption in his life through a deep and meaningful, ongoing, moment-by-moment sharing of his life with Jesus. If we also viewed the salvation of the mother whose daughter died as God's redemption of a consequence of sin – not the young woman's individual sin, but the consequence of living in a sin-based world where death still exists and the body is corrupted by that death from the moment of birth – thus death ultimately has "no sting" for either person. The daughter, because she is saved, is home with the Lord and living without suffering; and the mother, now saved, is alive for the first time.

I ask you to think on that last statement for just a moment: the mother is now alive for the first time. In reality, we are dead without Christ. But once we receive Him and His Spirit inhabits us, we become alive, *for the first time.* Our eternal life begins at that moment. We are not biding time waiting for heaven, nor are we laboring under a task or set of tasks that we must accomplish before we are permitted to begin an eternal existence. From the moment we receive Jesus, our lives are centered in that relationship with Him, and it is that relationship that gives us life. It is not that our physical lives do not matter to God. He created our physical bodies, He made us to be who we are, He gave us this world in which to live, so why would He create something worthless? However, it is true that, without Jesus, our spirits are dead, and "through Christ Jesus the law of the Spirit of life set me free from the law of sin and death (Romans 8:2)." When we accept Christ, "just as Christ was raised from the dead through the glory of the Father, we too may live a new life (Romans 6:4)." Notice that Paul does not say, "we too may now die and go to heaven." A later life is not the point; truly living now is the point. True life only comes in believing, receiving and then sharing your new life with Christ. This is what Paul means by the phrase, "to live is Christ."

Part of God's redemption of Cody's illness has been that Cody "can do everything through Him who gives [him] strength (Philippians 4:13)." Everything Cody has wanted to do, he has believed he could do because of God's presence and promise. If God did not value Cody's physical existence, why would He "make all things possible" for him? I have listed for you earlier some of Cody's many accomplishments, all of which were "impossible" if you asked anyone but Cody and Jesus. In fact, all of his doctors tell me his still being here with us now is "impossible." They can't figure it out, and call him the "miracle child." Do you believe that God did all this for some grand plan or agenda of His own, separate from Cody? Seeing us standing over Cody's hospital bed praying, reading the Bible, and laying our hands on Cody meant nothing to the doctors except the one who was already a Christian. The rest thought we were either silly or just in their way. They did not suddenly become believers when they witnessed Cody "miraculously" walking out of the hospital, something they had all said he would never do.

I am also not personally aware of any lives changing because Cody played football. I am aware, however, how much Cody enjoyed playing football, and how much it meant to Cody to receive the special recognition at the Tae Kwon Do Junior Olympics. I also know, because I know Jesus, how much He enjoyed sharing those life experiences with Cody. I am aware of the peace Cody had during his hospital stays, a peace that was way beyond anyone's understanding. In fact, one respiratory therapist thought Cody was unable to move because he lay so still and calm while she did some fairly painful procedures on him. When she asked us to help him slide up in the bed, and

Cody immediately slid himself into the position she wanted, she practically squealed in shock. Above all, I know the total intimacy Cody shares with Jesus each and every moment of his life. Isn't it much more likely that God made possible Cody's special accomplishments simply because God loves Cody? That Cody's life matters to God?

I am constantly amazed at how the same people, professing to worship the same God and know the same Savior that I know, can profess in one statement out of their mouths, "Jesus loved me so much He died for my sins," and in another statement out of the same mouths say, "it isn't about me," and somehow completely miss the contradiction in these two statements. However, we will fully discuss the current, and false, belief, "it isn't about me," in another chapter, so I will move on.

A part of the erroneous beliefs about suffering in the church arises from a misinterpretation of Romans 5:1-5. Prior to these verses, Paul has just presented an argument to support that we are justified through faith in Christ. He then continues:

> Therefore, since we have been justified through faith, we have peace with God through our Lord Jesus Christ, through whom we have gained access by faith into this grace in which we now stand. And we rejoice in the hope of the glory of God. Not only so, but we also rejoice in our sufferings, because we know that suffering produces perseverance; perseverance, character; and character, hope. And hope does not disappoint us, because God has poured our His love into our hearts by the Holy Spirit, whom He has given us. (Romans 5:1-5)

This section of Scripture has often been used to support the idea that God brings suffering to teach us lessons we need to learn, to "discipline" us, so to speak. However, nothing inherent or stated in these verses indicates God causes or brings the suffering. It is almost as if the church has written an understood but silent line at the beginning of verse 3: "because we know that [God produces suffering,] suffering produces perseverance…" and so on. However, this interpretation, besides making an assumption and adding to Paul's words, takes the words out of Paul's context. Notice that he begins with the peace we have with God, and the *access* we have to Him, to stand in His grace. This access is what I am describing, what I see each and every moment in Cody's life. It is through this *access* to God and through the love God has poured into our hearts and through the presence of the Holy Spirit in our lives that we are able to rejoice in our sufferings. God's redemption of our sufferings is then described, as Paul presents what God's grace and love and Spirit produce in us as He shares in our suffering and redeems it for us. Anyone who met Cody would say he has perseverance in excess (one of the awards he received at the Tae Kwon Do Junior Olympics was the "Perseverance Award"), that he has character even beyond most adults, and that he has boundless and apparently unrelenting hope. If you asked me where these qualities were produced, I would respond that God produced them in Cody through His redemption because of His great love for Cody, through the presence of His Spirit in Cody's heart, and, most of all, through the incredible intimacy Cody and Jesus share in their relationship. These are the qualities Paul is describing in his letter that grow out of our peace with God, and the joy we can have no matter what our circumstances may be.

So we are back now to the original questions of this section of the chapter: what is it that Cody has or Cody knows that alters his apparent struggles into great joy and peace? And how is it that Cody does not perceive himself as "suffering"? What

Cody has is a deep intimacy with Jesus. Cody does not walk through his days alone; he *could not*. Each and every moment is shared with Jesus. What Cody knows is that the kingdom of heaven is *now* and the kingdom of God is *within* him. When he has had a bad day and going to sleep could mean not waking up, his first move is to talk with Jesus and hear what He has to say on the matter. This one probably makes sense to most of you; of course, in the crisis times Cody would turn to Jesus. Cody shared with me that once, when he asked Jesus if he was going to die soon, Jesus responded, "touch as many lives as you can, then come on home." Cody said that this answer brought him great peace, knowing he wouldn't have to worry about the "when" and Jesus only wanted him to live each day fully.

But what about the other times, the easier times or better times? Every day, we take Cody on two "outings" to keep him moving, to get him exercise and to get his blood circulating and heart pumping valuable oxygen. Needless to say, in colder months, we wear out the local Wal Mart and Target stores. Their large space and wide aisles make it possible for Cody to wheel himself around fairly energetically. Most would call these activities "mundane," or even boring. However, Cody thoroughly enjoys them. He shares these outings with Jesus, in the same way that he shares his concerns, his questions and his struggles with Jesus. The joy is not found in the Target or Wal Mart, but in the company.

Chapter 8

Control or Sovereignty?

The Current State of the Church on God and Control

GOD IS IN CONTROL.

This statement is one I hear repeatedly from Christians, unilaterally spoken, without being questioned, as an absolute. The belief takes various forms in language and application, but it always boils down to this bottom-line: God is in control. To question this statement is to doubt the sovereignty, omnipotence, omniscience, and omnipresence of God, the Lordship of Christ, and the power of the Holy Spirit. Disagreeing with it is apparently the closest thing to blasphemy, short of denying the existence of God, that could be suggested to the church. It is foundational to virtually all sermons and studies. It is the often unspoken but always assumed precept underlying church theology across denominations. It is talked about, sung about, preached about and counted on as the Christian source of assurance and peace, and it is false.

Human beings seek security as a basic, fundamental, and fairly primitive need, just above physiological needs such as food, water, sleep and shelter on Maslow's Hierarchy of Needs. "God is in control" is a belief that addresses that basic need. If I believe in God and I assume He is in control, then I am secure. I am safe. It makes me feel good.

But what happens under that belief when something bad happens? My security is threatened; does that mean I cannot trust God? I am no longer safe; does that mean God no longer cares about me? Could it mean that God is distant and uninvolved? Is He angry with me? Could it mean that my safety and security are secondary to God's agenda? I have to find a plausible explanation for the terrible event, or my faith may be shaken; so I twist myself into a pretzel to try to make it make sense. "God is in control (without question); therefore, the bad thing that happened was:

1) part of God's master plan;
2) designed to teach me humility;
3) for a greater purpose that I don't see;
4) discipline because I am bad;
5) actually intended to keep me from some bigger trouble or disaster."

Exploration of the hidden assumptions that arise when these types of statements are drawn down to their logical conclusions does not occur, and "I have to have faith," is trotted out to cover over the problems in this mode of thinking. However, I will give voice here to the logical extensions that result from such statements:

1) I don't matter;
2) I am worthless;
3) God doesn't see or know me individually; my needs, wants or desires are irrelevant to Him, and He only cares about His agenda;
4) I am a shameful person, worthy of condemnation and unworthy of love;

5) God is a manipulator, or a chess master playing with my life, and I am just a pawn.

As I write these conclusions, I am reminding myself that some who are reading this will not recognize them as false. This unfortunate reality is a by-product of years of theology built upon a false foundation. Yes, I am claiming that God is not "in control." I also believe in God's authority, and that Jesus is our Sovereign Lord. When first reading these statements side by side, you may see them as contradictory; but we will demonstrate that they are not, and while you might assume in your perception of authority, sovereignty, and control that they have the same definition, we will show they do not. Hopefully, by the time this chapter is concluded, you will see that I am neither a blasphemer nor a heathen atheist for saying God is not "in control", and you will recognize such consequential beliefs as those listed above as patently false, and contrary to the "gospel" of Christ.

Historical Analysis

The only time that Paul mentions "control" in relation to God or Jesus is in his letter to the Philippians:

> But our citizenship is in heaven. And we eagerly await a Savior from there, the Lord Jesus Christ, who, *by the power that enables him to bring everything under his control,* will transform our lowly bodies so that they will be like his glorious body. (Philippians 3:20-21, italics added for emphasis)

In the context of this passage, Paul is discussing the coming judgment of God at the end of days. The eschatological and apocalyptic (in the sense of the end of the world) tones of Paul's theology are vital for the understanding of how Paul, and the early Christians, viewed the world in which they lived. We have already discussed how Mark, considered to be the earliest Gospel, contains a very apocalyptic undercurrent. However, as time passed and Jesus did not return to begin his judgment of mankind, even after Rome destroyed the Temple of Jerusalem, the imminence of Jesus' second coming and God's judgment began to be downplayed by the early Christians. Thus, Luke minimizes the eschatological nature of Jesus' teachings in his Gospel, and John has very little apocalyptic tone in his presentation of Jesus' message.[22]

Paul, however, was not part of the generation that began diminishing the imminence of the Apocalypse. Instead, Paul places great emphasis on the "day of God's wrath, when his righteous judgment will be revealed (Romans 2:5)." If you recall, part of Paul's "gospel" was the belief that Jesus would judge mankind at the end of the world. Just as Paul declares in the passage from Philippians that they are eagerly awaiting the day when Jesus returns, this section here shows his belief that God's righteous judgment had not yet been revealed, but would be. Currents of this apocalyptic belief flow throughout Paul's letters, manifesting themselves as statements expressed almost offhandedly. Paul seems to take God's judgment as a given, not spending any time expounding an argument to defend it as he does so many other issues. The fact that Paul did not see the need to convince his audience that the day was near reveals two things: that Paul assumed it was true, and that his audience assumed it was true. Instead Paul's assumptions about the Day of Judgment manifest themselves as short comments, such as, "the hour has come for you to wake up from your slumber, because our salvation is nearer now than when we first believed (Romans 13:11)." Paul even uses the assumption of the Apocalypse as evidence for his other contentions.

When arguing that people should not judge one another for their actions, Paul states "For we will all stand before God's judgment seat (Romans 14:10)." Thus his evidence for not passing judgment is the assumed truth that God will; a truth that Paul believed did not need any further explanation.

This belief of the nearness of the Day of Judgment actually prompted Paul to have to send a letter to the Thessalonians. The Thessalonians were apparently becoming agitated, because members among them had died and Jesus had not yet come back. Because the first generation had begun to grow old, the church was apparently worried about when and if Jesus would return, and what would happen to those who had already died when he did come back. Thus Paul has to calm the Thessalonians down:

> We believe that Jesus died and rose again and so we believe that God will bring with Jesus those who have fallen asleep in him…[W]e who are still alive, who are left till the coming of the Lord, will certainly not precede those who have fallen asleep. (I Thessalonians 4:14-15)

This explanation by Paul shows the Thessalonians' concern that their fellow believers are dying, but Jesus had not yet returned. It also clearly shows Paul's belief that Jesus would come back within their lifetimes, as he assumes that some of them will be "left till the coming of the Lord." Obviously Jesus did not return before Paul died. However, whether or not Paul was correct in his belief about the immediacy of the "Day of the Lord," as these examples illustrate, it was clearly a belief that he, as well as other early Christians, held.

Turning back now to the above passage from Philippians, the word that is translated "control" by the NIV (*hypotaxai*), is primarily a military term, meaning to place one in a lesser rank, or to compel subjection from someone. Thus, the use of "authority" or "subjection" would be a more accurate translation for this verse than "control," such as *by the power that enables him to bring everything under his authority* or *by the power that enables him to bring everything under his subjection.* Derivatives of the same word are used multiple times in a passage from Paul's letter to the church at Corinth, retaining their more militaristic connotations:

> Then the end will come, when [Jesus] hands over the kingdom to God the Father after he has destroyed all dominion, authority and power. For he must reign until he has put all his enemies under his feet. The last enemy to be destroyed is death. For he 'has put everything (*hypetaxen*) under his feet.' Now when it says that 'everything' has been put under him (*hypotetaktai*), it is clear that this does not include God himself, who put everything under (*hypotaxantos*) Christ. When he has done this (NIV translation; the Greek text restates the phrase, "When all things are subjected [*hypotage*] to him"), then the Son himself will be made subject (*hypotagesetai*) to him who put everything under him, so that God may be all in all. (I Corinthians 15:24-28)

As we have briefly discussed in a previous chapter, Paul viewed the world as being in the middle of a war, in which God and his agents fought against Satan and his agents. Thus, in Romans 13:12, Paul instructs the Christians to put on the "armor of light," as if they were engaging in battle. In the context of this belief, it makes sense that Paul would describe the end of the world in militaristic terms.

Thus, at the end battle, God would destroy every enemy and place everyone under his authority, saving those who had placed their faith in the "gospel" of Jesus' death and resurrection. God would climactically wrest authority in the world from the hands of his enemies, and Paul thought that it would happen within his generation. Paul does not question whether God has the power to enact these events. In fact, Paul's belief in the authority of God is a part of his assumption that Jesus would return and God would judge the world. But if the early Christians were waiting for the time in the future when God would place everything under his authority and subjection, then they must have, in the present, believed otherwise: that not everything was under God's authority and subjection. If Paul's apocalyptic theology is eagerly anticipating a future time when God would subject the world to his authority, then Paul must not have seen God as having "control" in the present.

If God's enemies were not presently subjected to His authority, as Paul stated in I Corinthians 15:24-28, and would not be until "the end," then what authority did Paul believe God's enemies had? In order to answer this question we need to turn back again to Paul's belief in a spiritual war. If God was in a war with Satan and his minions, and God was going to gain victoriously authority back at the end of this war, then he must have been battling Satan for "dominion, authority and power." This means that, for Paul, Satan presently had power in the world. Additionally, Paul attributed misfortunes and sufferings of the physical world to Satan and his agents. Thus, Paul's thorn was caused by an agent of Satan. Thus, the "false brothers" who were slandering Paul's reputation were agents of Satan. Thus, "Satan" prevented Paul from visiting the Thessalonians (I Thessalonians 2:18), probably through one or more of the travel hazards that Paul lists in II Corinthians. Thus, the "tempter" could have destroyed the faith of the Thessalonians through persecutions. Thus, Paul believed that Satan had power in the world, which was "under sin," because of Adam ("sin," as we have mentioned, being a supernatural force). In short, Paul believed that God and Satan were at war over the authority of this world until Jesus returned and "all things are subjected to him," when God crushed his enemies at the Last Judgment.

If Paul believed that Satan had power and authority on the earth, then what power did God wield? Paul talks repeatedly of power and authority given to him from God, authority for "building you [churches] up (II Corinthians 10:8, 13:10);" power of the gospel for the "salvation of everyone who believes (Romans 1:16);" power through "signs and miracles, through the power of the Spirit (Romans 15:9);" of his preaching "with a demonstration of the Spirit's power," rather than with "wise and persuasive words (I Corinthians 2:4);" and power as "weapons of righteousness in the right hand and the left (II Corinthians 6:7)." Especially through this final example, Paul's view of spiritual warfare shows itself once again. Paul believed that he and the other Christians were involved in the war, and God gave them weapons of warfare, "through the power of the Spirit." As Paul states, these Spirit weapons were not "the weapons of the world. On the contrary they have divine power... (II Corinthians 10:4)." What was this divine power? According to Paul, it was "...power to demolish strongholds. We demolish arguments and every pretension that sets itself up against the knowledge of God... (II Corinthians 10:4-5)." Paul's power, which came from the Spirit given by God, was the power to preach (I Corinthians 2:4) the gospel (Romans 1:16). This power took the form of debate and discourse, demolishing arguments and pretensions, which, as we have seen, Paul attributed multiple times to the power of the Spirit. God then essentially armed his soldiers fighting against strongholds of argument and pretension with the divine weapons of language, and "signs and miracles." In other words, God gave Paul and the apostles the power to influence other people, to reveal truth, and to break down pretenses, lies, and deceptions.

Restored State of God and Choice

As I stated earlier in this chapter, many of the terms used by the church to talk about God being in control, His sovereignty, and His authority are used interchangeably and thought to mean the same things. They are not interchangeable, however, so I will begin with a clarification and defining of all of the relevant terms.

The actual dictionary definition of "control" is "to exercise restraining or directing influence over." This definition sounds very much like authority, which means both "power to influence thought or behavior," and "right," as in a person's right to lead. However, this definition of "control" is not how the word is utilized or meant in our common language usage, or in the church, today. The connotation given to "control" in today's language is the removal of choice. I say this based on an acute awareness that the church does not in any way view God as influencing, but sees Him instead as determining. To "determine" means "to fix conclusively" and "to fix the form or character of." It also means, "to be the cause of or reason for." Clearly, "control" as used today has more of an implication of determination than one of influence. Thus, for the purposes of this discussion, the word "control" will be defined as "to determine or fix," with the understanding that control includes the concept of the removal of choice.

Satan's "authority" on this earth, based as stated above on the world being "under sin," is "the power to influence thought or behavior." God, also, has "authority," defined as both "the power to influence thought or behavior" and "the right" to this influence. Satan's power is through usurped authority, meaning he has the power, but not the right, to influence thought or behavior. Therefore, Satan is not sovereign, whereas God, as the Creator, has genuine authority over His creation and the right to exercise this power to influence thought or behavior. Thus He is sovereign. "Sovereign" is defined as "the right to rule" and "one possessing supreme or highest authority."

Sovereign is a term that describes God's position as Lord, but does not include any connotation of control. A king, for example, is in the position of supreme authority in his country. He has the right to rule in authority, but does not, as a result, have the ability to control his subjects. In other words, he cannot "fix conclusively" their obedience to his authority. While he may attempt to gain measures of control through various methods, such as keeping a standing police force or executing anyone who disagrees with him, he still cannot force obedience from all of his subjects. There will always be those who refuse to obey, and this type of behavior, attempting to completely control the population, has led to many despots and just as many tragedies. Thus, to reiterate, authority, as defined above, means the power to influence, not the ability to control. The king may be the highest authority, with the greatest influence, but again without the ability to control. The citizens who are subject under him still have the choice to either obey or disobey his influence. The same is true of God's sovereignty, and claiming otherwise is tantamount to calling God a tyrannical despot.

In light of these definitions, Paul's description of God removing Satan's power and authority at "the end" makes much more sense. It also clarifies Paul's belief in the ongoing nature of spiritual warfare in which we as followers of Christ are engaged. If God is in control, why is there a war? If, however, we view the war as God's sovereign authority clashing against Satan's usurped authority, or as God's ability to influence with truth and love, from His position of having the right to rule and highest authority, versus Satan's power to influence through deception and manipulation from his position as the legal authority over lies, then we are able to see that we have choices to make, and how our choices effect outcomes.

With the terms defined, let's briefly revisit the consequences of the false belief that God is in control listed in the introduction of this chapter. They were:

1) I don't matter;
2) I am worthless;
3) God doesn't see or know me individually; my needs, wants or desires are irrelevant to Him, and He only cares about His agenda;
4) I am a shameful person, worthy of condemnation and unworthy of love;
5) God is a manipulator, or a chess master playing with my life, and I am just a pawn.

First, and most obvious, is that none of these five statements carries even the hint of a loving relationship. In fact, quite the opposite is true. Not only is love absent from the equation, the attitudes and character that these responses ascribe to God are actually more in line with the enemy's nature. So, for example, if we were to give a visual image to the statement "God is a chess master and I am just a pawn," we would most likely see someone chuckling calculatingly over the world, rubbing his hands together in anticipation of his next "move," reaching out to manipulate the pieces into position, and unfolding his master strategy to win his game. He would be happily sacrificing pieces toward his objective of winning but certainly never seeing, feeling for, or caring about the pieces he was moving and losing. Is that a picture that you can see with Jesus in the role of the chess player? Does this image match, in any way, anything about the character of Christ as reflected in Scripture? Is this the attitude and behavior we are called to emulate? Paul asks the question in this way: "What harmony is there between Christ and Belial (Satan)? (II Corinthians 6:15)."

Next, we need to realize that these beliefs are opposed to Paul's beliefs and teaching, and therefore divergent from the writings we have that are closest to the original teaching of Christ and the earliest beliefs of the church. According to Paul:

> ...you received a spirit of sonship. And by him we cry, 'Abba, Father.' The Spirit Himself testifies with our spirit that we are God's children. Now if we are children, then we are heirs – heirs of God and co-heirs with Christ. (Romans 8:15- 17).

Also, "So from now on we regard no one from a worldly point of view...Therefore, if anyone is in Christ, he is a new creation; the old has gone, the new has come! (II Corinthians 5:16-17)." And again, "You are all sons of God through faith in Christ Jesus, for all of you who were baptized into Christ have clothed yourselves with Christ (Galatians 3:26)." And, "we...are being transformed into his likeness with ever-increasing glory, which comes from the Lord, who is the Spirit (II Corinthians 3:18)." It is difficult to imagine God, our Father, seeing us, His children, as worthless or unimportant, and it makes no sense at all that He would make us a new creation but that creation not matter to Him, or that He would not care about those who are clothed with Christ or being transformed into the likeness of His Son. Would Jesus "die for all (II Corinthians 5:15)" if all were worthless and didn't matter to Him? Additionally, Paul states, "...those who live in accordance with the Spirit have their minds set on what the Spirit desires (Romans 8:5)." This teaching stands in direct conflict to any idea that God does not care about my desires, because those desires are in fact His desires if His Spirit lives within me. In regards to shame, Romans 8:1 removes any question: "Therefore, there is now no condemnation for those who are in Christ Jesus, because through Christ Jesus the law of the Spirit of life set me free from the law of sin and death." So, Christ Jesus has set us free from shame.

Finally, we need to see how, starting from a false foundation, the more we build onto that foundation, the farther removed we are from any aspect of the truth of God and the more deceived we become. Take as an example Paul's' description of love:

> Love is patient, love is kind. It does not envy, it does not boast, it is not proud. It is not rude, it is not self-seeking, it is not easily angered, it keeps no records of wrongs. Love does not delight in evil but rejoices with the truth. It always protects, always trusts, always hopes, always perseveres. Love never fails. (I Corinthians 13: 4-8).

The false belief, "God is in control," leads us to assumptions about the character of God and our relationship with Him that are 180 degrees apart from these verses. Suddenly, God is completely self-seeking, proud, and rude; He is neither patient with us nor kind to us; He does not protect us but instead uses us for His own ends; and, He delights in evil things such as manipulation and condemnation, and cares nothing for our own despair.

I have seen the consequences of these beliefs in my counseling office on a daily basis. Such problematic issues as severe depression, debilitating anxiety, and even suicidal ideation grow from these conclusions. To say that "I am worthless" is an unhealthy belief would be a gross understatement. Feeling used, powerless and trapped, and unloved and unimportant are feelings no one wants to experience; they are painful and damaging. Does this sound like love, or God, to you?

Belief in "control" is a destructive belief. We have already explored briefly how control in the macrocosm of government and society is harmful, potentially leading to despotism. Adolf Hitler is a clear example of the consequences of control at this level of rule. Six million people died at the directive of this one man. Yet, in spite of his attempts at complete control, there were still individuals who stood against him and who, in spite of the consequences to themselves, refused to obey him. One noted Christian who did so, at the cost of his own life, was Dietrich Bonhoeffer. Inside Germany, both before and during World War II, Bonhoeffer openly opposed Nazism and Hitler's anti-Semitic policies. Hitler is one example out of innumerable dictators whose attempts at control led to horror, and who demonstrate the destructive nature of control on a societal level. But what about on the personal level?

In the microcosm, within each individual, control is just as destructive. As indicated above, the results of control, feeling powerless and trapped, are the breeding ground beliefs for depression and anxiety disorders. Interpersonally, divorce is most often related to control; either one spouse trying to control the other, or one feeling controlled by the other. Control is the underlying issue beneath fights over money, sex, poor communication, and daily living concerns such as roles in the marriage. Several personality disorders have, at their heart, control as a symptom or a response. Eating disorders stem from a desire to control some aspect of one's life. Sexual abuse, rape, child abuse and spousal abuse are all rooted in power and control issues.

So here is the bottom line: control is an enemy concern. "It is for freedom that Christ has set us free (Galatians 5:1)," not for control. Control carries with it one additional problem: if you agree with "in control," then "out of control" must also follow as a possibility. What I mean is that control, like many such beliefs, is like a coin; it has two sides. Someone who controls by definition can also be out of control. At any given moment, the heads can flip to tails, and the controlling individual is suddenly spinning out of control. This two-sided fruit of one belief is also seen in such enemy issues as pride, which is Satan's sin according to the stories of the Old Testament. If I am prideful, I will also have self-abasement and a sense of being nothing. If I can be the most, then I can also be the least. It is only a question of which side of the coin is in evidence at any given time. Therefore, when we say, "God is in control," we are also stating that God can be out of control. The truth is, then, that control is not of God or from God. Instead, choice, as given to us when God gave us free will, is God's alternative to control.

Some may say that the absence of control is the same thing as chaos, which is not of God: "For God is not a God of disorder but of peace (I Corinthians 14:33)." However, "in control" and "disorder/out of control" are actually opposite sides of the same "coin." It is correct that disorder or being out of control is no more a part of God's truth than controlling is; both are on the same continuum, just on opposite ends of it. In order not to deal in that "continuum" of the enemy, God created us on a different continuum, which is freedom of choice. This is the reason why control does not exist in our reality. When He gave us free will, He removed the power of control, on both ends of the continuum. Satan entices us to try to control, which does not and cannot work, or he deceives us into feeling out of control, through perceived disorder and chaos in our lives or in the world. Either way, if we choose to agree, he has suckered us into believing in his continuum, and thereby abdicating our God-given position of freedom. I am making the point here that, even in the realm of Satan's deception about control, *we still have a choice!* Free will, our freedom to choose, is a card that trumps all of the enemy's power. We can *choose* to believe in Jesus Christ as our Lord and Savior, we can *choose* to follow the leading of the Holy Spirit in all aspects of our lives, we can *choose* to "...not gratify the desires of the sinful nature (Galatians 5:14)," we can *choose* to live in the truth of God. In so doing, "We demolish arguments and every pretension that sets itself up against the knowledge of God, and we take captive every thought to make it obedient to Christ (II Corinthians 10:5)."

Do you see how, in order to equip and strengthen us in the fight against evil and to effectively partner with us in that war, God behaved in a way that would appear paradoxical to us? He Who is the sovereign authority gave freedom to those He created, which meant He *shared* that authority instead of wielding it over us, knowing that sharing it was the way to regain it. Where our worldly response to someone usurping our authority would be to try to grab for control, God responds by relinquishing control and giving freedom. Through giving authority to His children, God has given us the weapon needed to defeat the enemy's power in this world, even though sin still exists in this earthly plane. For what can Satan do if we choose God?

156

As stated in the historical section of this chapter, Paul attributes the power to destroy strongholds and demolish the deceptions of the enemy to the Holy Spirit, saying it is "divine power (II Corinthians 10:4)." Thus, we are partners with God, by God's choice and design. We teach or preach the truth, and His Spirit gives those words the power to persuade. We argue against the enemy's deceptions, and it is His Spirit that empowers us to influence other people, and His Spirit Who reveals all truth. When our actions and choices reflect the presence (fruit - Galatians 5:22) of His Spirit in our lives, those "signs and wonders" begin to break down the enemy's pretenses, lies, deceptions, and strongholds (I am not saying those are the only signs of the Spirit's power. Paul did clearly believe in the manifestations of the Gifts of the Spirit, such as prophecy and speaking in tongues, as he addresses them in I Corinthians and Romans).

I have described our partnership with God in warfare against evil in this way: if I build my own castle, no matter how high the walls appear, my enemy is already inside my walls, wreaking havoc and destruction, and he can have his way with me. However, if God builds my castle through His Spirit bringing truth into my heart, our enemy is outside those walls. Jesus and I stand together on the ramparts, the "high ground," which is every warrior's favorite site, using the divine weapons He has provided me to crush our enemy's fortifications from afar. It is easier to deal with an enemy whose position is a column of smoke in a distant field than one who has brought all of his weapons and soldiers inside your castle.

Spiritual warfare is not the only area of our lives where God partners with us. It is His desire to partner with us in *all* aspects of our lives. Some, or even most, believers are fairly comfortable with the idea of God being a part of their spiritual lives. They expect Him to be their focus during church, they may be willing to turn to Him in times of great need or crisis, and some of them choose to include Him in designated times of Bible study and/or prayer during the week. However, few believers talk about or experience walking through each and every day, all day long, with Jesus as their companion. We try instead to compartmentalize Him into only the spiritualized aspects of living, and leave Him out of the day-to-day. As a result, we do not perceive or expect Him to act as a partner with us. Instead, we call on Him like we call the plumber when our drains clog or our washers start leaking. I'm not sure any of us would describe our relationship with the local plumber as intimate, or as a partnership. We just want the plumber to fix the mess and leave as quickly as possible, right?

Yet, Paul suggests something very different from such a business arrangement when he writes, "Be joyful *always*; pray *continually*; give thanks in *all circumstances*, for this is God's will for you in Christ Jesus (I Thessalonians 5:16-18);" and, "Rejoice in the Lord *always*…Do not be anxious for anything, but in *everything*, by prayer and petition, with thanksgiving, present your requests to God. And the peace of God, which transcends all understanding, will guard your hearts and your minds in Christ Jesus (Philippians 4:4,6-7)" (italics added for emphasis). Repeatedly, Paul teaches that God is involved with us in all of our circumstances, in all things, always, continually, and in everything. He also writes that living in this type of relationship with Jesus is God's will, and that God's peace will guard our hearts and minds as a result. Basically, Paul is stating this type of intimate living, with Jesus as our partner in all things, is preferable to any other alternative. Notice also Paul's emphasis on prayer in this process of partnership.

Unfortunately, in this sin-based world, the time *will* come for all of us when we need the assurance of an intimate partner. I question if, in the middle of the crises, an unknown or barely familiar businessperson responding is what we really need or want? If instead, we desire someone we already know intimately, and that we already trust, when we are in need, I suggest that developing intimacy and partnership with Jesus on an ongoing, day-to-day basis, as Paul suggests, is much more efficacious than trying to find it or start one somehow in the middle of the crisis or in the time of our greatest need. If we live in that type of relationship with Christ, we will know it and be able to rely on it when we need it most; *and*, we will be able to enjoy the sharing of it in all things.

I have been asked many times, more times than I can count, how it is that I am "handling" my son, Cody's, illness, his brushes with death, his repeated hospitalizations, and his degeneration and poor prognosis. Most people who ask me this question follow it up with the assertion that they could not handle it. I'm not either, is the honest answer. I am not one of those Christians who believes that I "should" (note the shame-based word here, which is one reason I reject this belief) put on a happy-Jesus face to prove something to others about God's ability to deal with death and loss, for this is done in my own effort and is a pretense which proves nothing at all about God. I have shed tears in my Sunday school class, I have wept in grief and in anger in Cody's hospital room, and I have been not-so-nice to a doctor or respiratory therapist or two who have tried to do things or who said things that we disagreed with in front of Cody. Nor am I one of those Christians who believes (the unstated belief: God is in control, therefore) everything will work out according to God's will, so I pretend to myself and others that everything will be just fine, and live in denial, never truly dealing with what is happening. I wake up each morning and go to sleep each night dealing with the reality that any moment could be Cody's last; it could be the last time I hear his laugh, or the last time that I can touch his face or hands, or the last time that his sweet singing will wake me up in the morning.

My honest answer is that if Jesus was not my intimate partner, and if I had not already had that kind of relationship with Him when this crisis started, I don't know what I would have done or how I could have survived it to this point. Cody's amazingly positive attitude and incredible strength have been examples for me, but I know where those things come from in him: he shares a deep intimacy with Jesus that is beyond compare.

Cody and I share reliance on Jesus as our partner, in this time of great need and in all things. If it appears to others that I am "strong," as it appears to me that Cody is strong, then it is Christ with me they are seeing, just as it is Christ with Cody that I see. I don't want or need a controlling "God" to manage or change my circumstances for me. I need a loving partner who will stand with me and hold me and comfort me and support me, no matter what my circumstances are. I don't want to pray to some distant, dictatorial, above-it-all Chess Master and try to do the right song and dance for him to snap his scheming fingers and fix this. In particular, I don't want to go to some manipulative User who, according to the "God is in control" belief, caused Cody's illness to begin with, and beg Him to do something about it just to make Himself look good. I need someone Who loves me, Who I can talk to, and cry *with*, and Who truly understands how I am feeling and shares the pain of it with me. I need someone Who will speak words of truth to me, Who can honestly remind me that I am not alone, Who will help me to see when I cannot see, and Who will stand by me when I am at my weakest and most vulnerable. I need my Jesus.

Chapter 9

Works or Partnership?

The Current State of the Church on Works and Self-Reliance

THERE SEEMS TO BE A PREVALENT BELIEF AMONG CHRISTIANS that the saying, "God helps those who help themselves," comes from the Bible. It does not. The phrase has been attributed to Ben Franklin as well, but actually predates him, going back at least to Aesop. However, many Christians today accept this statement as Scriptural.[23] It is certainly in line with American cultural values. However, Paul's teachings, as recorded in the seven undisputed letters we have as a part of our Bible, directly contradict the idea of self-reliance.

Perhaps the United States is an untrusting culture at its core. Perhaps our "pioneer" spirit has been passed down through the generations, and "pulling ourselves up by our own bootstraps" remains the code we follow. Perhaps our society is so based in independence, or we are simply a rebellious people, and cannot bear the thought of relying on someone else. No matter what the reason is for this cultural ideal, we do have it, and we believe in it deeply. It is certainly understandable, then, that our discomfort with dependence on another would translate into our relationship with God. However, the consequences to us for that transference are severe.

Of course, upon a superficial examination, this saying seems to make sense to us; after all, it agrees with our already-held beliefs and values. For us to accommodate for an opposite belief would be too difficult. So, we place God in the American box, claim that God loves freedom, equate freedom with independence, correlate independence with self-reliance, and arrive at our conclusion that God leaves it up to us. This progression seems both logical and comfortable to us, and we embrace it enthusiastically, forgetting, as did the Corinthians apparently, the very heart of the "gospel":

> Now, brothers, I want to remind you of the gospel I preached to you, which you received and on which you have taken your stand. *By this gospel you are saved*, if you hold firmly to the word I preached to you...that Christ died for our sins according to the Scriptures...(I Corinthians 15:1-3, italics added for emphasis).

Paul's entire argument on grace is based on the truth that we cannot save ourselves, for if we could save ourselves, there would have been no need for Christ to die for our sins.

The initial premise is true: God loves freedom. Our misstep in logic occurs at the next statement, which assumes freedom and independence mean the same thing. Going back briefly to the concepts of the previous chapter, freedom indicates an internal state of being that means we have a choice, that we have been released from or are not suffering, and that there is no such thing for us as "control." Independence refers to not being affiliated with a larger controlling body, as in self-governing, or not relying on something or someone else. Restated, independence is defined in how we relate to others while freedom is defined within ourselves. This difference is how Paul can be free while in chains, yet would not be considered independent while he was in prison under the apparent "control" of the Roman government. As we have discussed before, an incorrect premise invalidates the logic of the argument. We cannot, therefore, draw the conclusion that since God loves freedom, God leaves everything up to us.

In addition to negating the gospel and confusing our thinking, a third consequence arises from transferring independence into our beliefs about our relationship with God, and this consequence may be the most damaging. Viewed through the lens of this belief, God is a distant, uninvolved, and uncaring Father. Two images come to mind. The first is of the father who arrives home late in the day to hear about the misadventures of his children from the mom, who has told the children "wait until your father gets home" and who gives the father strict instructions to carry out the proper punishment. This father's interaction with his children consists of scolding or spanking, frustration and anger. The children learn they can do nothing that pleases their dad, and they will never be good enough. The second image is of the "Disney dad" as noncustodial fathers are sometimes called, or the traveling salesman father who is only home on the occasional weekend. These fathers don't want anything negative to mar their extremely limited time with their children, so they forego discipline and become the "rescuers" who give in to all their children's demands, but who are completely uninvolved in the day-to-day of their children's lives. They want desperately to be seen as the "good guys," but end up being seen as a giant wallet, with no respect or depth of relationship at all. None of these examples would be considered to have a healthy relationship with their children, from a psychological standpoint.

Applying these images to God, He becomes either the Great Punisher from Above who sends lightning bolts down on us when we mess up, or the Great Watcher from Afar who sweeps in at the last second for His own glory and purposes (if we beg Him of course), to get us out of a problem we have created for ourselves, but only after we have tried and tried again to get ourselves out of it and failed. Both outlooks include a strong element of annoyance and frustration with us. The first aggravation is obvious: "You messed it all up again, you bad child; shame on you!" The second, not quite so overt, looks like, "Because I am so wonderful and awesome, I'll get you out of this mess, *again*; but can't you handle anything without me having to jump in there to fix it for you, you failure?" In both cases, feelings of shame and inadequacy result from this imagined interaction, and distancing and loss of trust consume our perception of God.

Out of this alienation from God through our own misperception of Who He is grows yet another consequence to us. As often happens in children who feel inadequate and shamed before their parent, we begin to try to earn His positive attention. "Maybe if I can be good enough, God will accept me," we begin to believe. We develop a "works" mentality. While from one side of our mouths we profess "saved by grace through faith," out of the other side comes the list of "things we have to do." Christian self-help books (shouldn't this be an oxymoron?) are ready and willing to offer us a plethora of "lists of six": "six habits for successful" this and "seven steps to the best possible" that. Whenever I see the movie, *Snow White*, and hear the song of the dwarves where they chant, "We work work work work work work work work work the whole day through," I think of church members. Self-effort and self-reliance are thereby reinforced in us from two sides, from both our cultural beliefs and the multiple layers of consequences from those beliefs. Quite a trap set by the enemy for us, isn't it?

Historical Analysis

Paul, in his letter to the Thessalonians, states:

Make it your ambition to lead a quiet life, to mind your own business and to work with your hands, just as we told you, so that your daily life may win the respect of outsiders and *so that you will not be dependent on anybody.* (I Thessalonians 4:11-12, italics added for emphasis)

According to this statement, Paul was telling his churches to be independent. It is ridiculous to assume, however, that Paul held himself to the 21st century American cultural values of independence or the "self made man." Thus, it is a safe assumption that his definition of independence would be different from those of a person in this century with our social context. We have discussed Paul's social context, but when he urges his church to be independent in this letter, what did he mean? For Paul, this "independence" is related to physical work, probably associated with maintaining financial autonomy. Paul explains earlier in his letter, "Surely you remember, brothers, our toil and hardship; we worked night and day in order not to be a burden to anyone while we preached the gospel of God to you (1 Thessalonians 2:9)." In other words, Paul worked a job while he was preaching in Thessalonica, in order to not be dependent on a member of the town for support during his visit. If he was urging the rest of the church to do as he instructed, this probably included imitation of his actions while he was in the town (i.e. working and not being in debt to another member of the town).

Paul seems to make no connection, however, between not being financially dependent on anybody, and self-reliance in spiritual righteousness. As we have discussed, Paul attributes all of his power, the "signs and wonders," his teaching, the ability to destroy arguments and deceit, joy in the midst of persecution, power in weakness, and even the fact that he is able to be an apostle, to reliance on God and God's Spirit. How is it, though, that he can urge people to be independent, yet at the same time to be completely dependent on God? This is because, as Paul seems to do in many matters, he draws a distinction between the physical and the spiritual. Paul sees a difference between physical independence and spiritual freedom, and we will turn back to this issue shortly.

When discussing religious matters, Paul seems to object strongly to the ability to gain righteousness through independent effort, and he uses the Jewish law as an example of this. Multiple times, in regards to Paul's discussion of "faith" and "works," Paul equates the law with trying to obtain righteousness through one's own personal effort, which he places in opposition to righteousness by faith. Thus he states, "The law is not based on faith. On the contrary, 'The man who does these things will live by them' (Galatians 3:12)." Additionally, Paul describes "not having a righteousness of *my own* that comes from the law, but that which is through faith in Christ (Philippians 3:9, italics added)." Paul describes this attempt at independent exertion as ineffective:

> Israel, who pursued a law of righteousness, has not attained it [righteousness]. Why not? Because they pursued it not by faith but as if it were by works. (Romans 9:31-32)

He further explains, "if a law had been given that could impart life, then righteousness would certainly have come by the law (Galatians 3:21)." This contrary-to-fact statement can be extended to include Paul's implied conclusion, "But in fact there is no such law, so righteousness cannot come by any law." As we have seen several times in our analysis, both in previous chapters and here, Paul vehemently believes and argues that people cannot gain righteousness through the Jewish law. Seeing now that Paul equated observance of the law with independent attempts to pursue righteousness through "works," Paul thus argues that righteousness cannot be gained through independent effort. In other words, since Paul equated the law with independent works, and he placed the law in opposition to faith, he clearly saw works as oppositional to faith.

This takes us back now to Paul's discussion of independence and dependence. Paul creates a dichotomy between "independence" and "freedom." He urges the Thessalonian church to work hard so as "not to be dependent on anybody," yet he also explains that salvation comes through faith in Jesus ("faith," as we have seen, being used according to Paul's conceptual framework, and in opposition to independent works). Paul's "independence," therefore, most likely related to financial self-sufficiency and not being indebted as members of the church. Additionally, Paul begins his list of "sufferings" in II Corinthians with the declaration, "I have worked much harder… (II Corinthians 11:23)." This inclusion directly relates hard work with the rest of the list of physical sufferings, and hard work is unrelated to "works" in regards to the spiritual.

However, to Paul, where "independence" relates to the physical world, "freedom" relates to spiritual matters. When Paul exclaims, "It is for freedom that Christ has set us free (Galatians 5:1)," what is he talking about? When discussing spiritual freedom, Paul draws a paradoxical dichotomy between freedom and slavery. He explains to the Roman church, "When you were slaves to sin, you were free from righteousness (Romans 6:20; the NIV adds 'free from [the control of] righteousness' but this phrase is not in the original Greek)." However, he explains, "...you have been set free from sin and become slaves to God (Romans 6:22)." Thus, Paul regards "freedom" from sin as "slavery" to God, and "slavery" to sin as "freedom" from righteousness. In other words, the "freedom" of which Paul speaks is actually slavery, still on the same coin, still dependence upon something. When slaves to sin and free from righteousness, people were still dependent on the sway of sin. When slaves to God and righteousness, people are free from sin yet still dependent on God. While Paul may equate physical independence as not relying on others, he clearly viewed spiritual "freedom" as being manifested through "slavery," dependence on something else.

For Paul, it was belief that held weight and allowed one to gain this paradoxical "freedom" through slavery. Thus he declares, "If you ...believe in your heart that God raised him [Jesus] from the dead, you will be saved. For it is with your heart that you believe and are justified (Romans 10:9-10)." It is important now to recall our previous analysis of how Paul uses the Greek *pistis*. This word is translated as both "faith" and "belief" (and a list of other words) by the NIV, hinting at minor differences that readers of English place on the words and their contexts. However, we have already examined how Paul conceptualized faith, belief, and the whole other host of English words employed by the NIV to encompass the meaning of *pistis*: firm persuasion by hearing the gospel, leading to the trust that God is trustworthy in his promise, causing a calling out and surrender to God. According to this statement then, Paul taught that people are "justified" and "saved" when they believe (by hearing, etc.) that Jesus was raised from the dead (Paul's gospel). In other words, when Paul argues that Abraham was fully persuaded by God's promise and was "justified" and seen as righteous before God by "faith," it is in the same way that Paul contends people are "justified" by "faith" in the gospel of Jesus' resurrection. They are convinced or persuaded through hearing which results in the rest of the conceptual matrix.

Furthermore, according to Paul's theology, "the Spirit of him who raised Jesus from the dead is living in you (Romans 8:11)." Of this Spirit, Paul also explains, "God has poured out his love into our hearts by the Holy Spirit, whom he has given us (Romans 5:5)." Finally, it was through this same Spirit that Paul believed he was able to be an apostle and have the power to persuade people (resulting in persuasion and "belief") and destroy arguments and deceit. In other words, Paul described a cycle of faith that depended on God's power. The only way Paul believed he had the power to persuade others to "believe" was through God's Spirit, and this Spirit came directly from God, as a result of one's belief. The Spirit of God pours into and resides in one's heart, giving power, as a result of belief coming from one's heart.

If Paul also declares "…where the Spirit of the Lord is, there is freedom (II Corinthians 3:17)," this shows that he clearly attributes "freedom" to God's Spirit as well, the same Spirit that gives him power, and the one he teaches is gained through the belief that "…Christ has set us free" through death and resurrection. Thus, we are back to the beginning of this discussion: that Paul taught his churches that belief in his gospel brought about "freedom" by dependence on the actions of Jesus, when he justified mankind before God through his death and resurrection. This is a lengthy, circuitous discussion, yet it is a very important understanding to grasp. This whole series of steps can be summed up with a simple statement: it was belief or faith that allowed one to gain "freedom" through Paul's paradoxical explanation of becoming a slave to God.

Restored State of Spirit-Centered Partnership

True freedom comes from dependence on and reliance on God. This statement, as shown above, is in agreement with Paul's views as presented in his writing. It is also human nature to swing from extreme to extreme, rather than to move to another plane of understanding. In this case, a swing to an extreme might be to conclude, "Since I am totally dependent on God, then I will just sit around and wait on Him to do everything for me." However, this statement is not in line with Paul's teachings, and continues to maintain an external point of view contrary to how we have discussed spiritual freedom. If freedom is an *internal* state of being rather than an *external* gaining or losing of control, then to truly understand and experience the freedom that Jesus Christ has for us, we must move from the external plane to the internal plane. In other words, we stop doing for the sake of doing, or *not* doing for the sake of not doing, and move to living in our true state of being.

So what is our true state of being? According to Paul, we are spiritual creatures, with our "flesh" or "sinful nature" having died with Christ on the cross, and our resurrection with Christ occurring through living "by the Spirit" (Romans 6-8, Galatians 5):

> Those who live according to the sinful nature have their minds set on what that nature desires; but those who live in accordance with the Spirit have their minds set on what the Spirit desires. The mind of sinful man is death, but the mind of the Spirit is life and peace (as before, the

NIV adds "the mind [controlled by] the Spirit," which is not present in the original Greek)...You, however, are not in the flesh but in the Spirit (NIV, "controlled not by the sinful nature but by the Spirit," but again, this is not representative of the Greek), if the Spirit of God lives in you. And if anyone does not have the Spirit of Christ, he does not belong to Christ. But if Christ is in you, your body is dead because of sin, yet *your spirit is alive* because of righteousness. (Romans 8:5-6, 9-10).

Paul is describing living in the internal reality of our spirit's resurrection in the now: note the use of the present tense when Paul states, "your spirit *is* alive." He is not talking about some future event when we die and rise to meet Jesus in heaven, as if our life in the Spirit is "on hold" until that day. We are one with the Spirit of Christ *now*. Any belief that separates us from God, whether it is a belief in our own sufficiency and self-reliance, or our abdication to God's "control," is false. In other words, if I see God as "out there" or "over there" while I view myself as in the center of things in my life (it doesn't matter if I see myself as directing my own life or sitting around waiting on God to do so, I am still the center of my universe from my perspective...it is still self-centered), then I am not living from the truth of my state of being. This truth is: I am no longer a "me;" I am now an "us."

If I live from that external perspective on God, then I will try to "pull" righteousness into myself; thus, I will *do* those things I believe are righteous in order to gain righteousness within. This is exactly backwards. As with many deceptions of the enemy, it appears on the surface to be a reasonable response, but it ends up 180 degrees from the truth. As I attempt to gain righteousness by pulling it into myself from some external source such as my own actions, I grab huge chunks of worldliness at the same time and pull those things opposed to Christ into me. If I live in the external, I become of the world. For example, motivated by a desire to be a good Christian and do what God tells me to do, I volunteer at the homeless shelter, but my heart is not really for the homeless or meeting their needs. Instead, it is my own desire to be "good." What I can come away with is a sense of my own importance, a self-righteous pride that "puffs me up" and tells me "I did good" so God will be proud of me. "Well done, good and faithful servant" is interpreted as "you are acceptable now" in my heart, and I become like the Pharisee described in the parable who prays *about himself* and says "God, I thank you that I am not like other men (Luke 18:9-14)." Do you see the "I" focus in this story?

I have observed over the years that Christianity seems to go through "phases" much like fashion trends or popular musical styles. It was not just during the first centuries that Jesus and Christian theologies were molded to fit into various social contexts, nor is it isolated to this generation.[24] I remember back when I was a sixties child hearing the "Jesus freaks," who didn't seem to talk very differently from the hippies. Later, during a period of extreme social consciousness, there was a focus on "being the hands and feet of Jesus," where all the campus religious groups spent their free time in the inner city talking to the youth and planning "fun" activities for the poor underprivileged "others" of society (trying to include them as if they were seen as a part of society yet still singled out as those "outside" who needed our help). Now, in response to the "extreme" trend that has become popular to American culture today (just take a look at advertising), Christianity has taken on the personality of the X-Games, the word "awesome" has become synonymous with God, and pastors rappel from the rafters to deliver their messages like Garth Brooks in concert (I'm not making this up). Churches build skate parks on their grounds for the "skater" youth, and Jacuzzi baptismal pools with flashing colored lights for the "cool" adults. Everything is "extreme" and "for His glory." We "lift our hands" for His glory, we "sing praise" for His glory, we "worship" for His glory, we "shout and dance and beat the drums and play guitar and entertain the 'unchurched'" for His glory... because He is "so awesome." Over the centuries, in response to changing social contexts, church services have covered the spectrum from household gatherings to sacrosanct rituals to rock concerts, depending on the cultural trends of the society at the time. This is not an attack on any particular style of church service or ritual, but can you see how the church has *reflected* culture instead of *transforming* it? These are examples of living in and from the external realm and therefore becoming a part of the world.

Another example is the focus in church today on numbers: the larger the congregation, the greater the pastor's security (and the higher his salary). Churches become managed like the local Starbuck's, complete with coffee houses and bookstores within their walls. Church services are designed according to marketing strategies, and business plans have replaced the presence of the Holy Spirit and the prayers of church members in directing the path of the church. Of course, all of this is disguised under the heading, "How to reach more people." I wonder, though, how well those "newly reached" people are discipled in Christ once they are captured under the roof. My observation has been that they are not. Instead, general sermons preached to a congregation of hundreds or thousands, or small groups that become social events led by equally uncertain young believers, are relied upon to teach the new Christians. Is it any wonder the church is seen by those outside of it (even some believers) as superficial and meaningless?

I hear a lot of Christians talk about living "authentic" lives, but I am not sure what they mean when they say that. Some people seem to be talking about living up to some "list of six" that have I mentioned several times; "getting it right," in other words. Some are referring to being honest about their failings, while some are speaking of correctly following the law. Quite honestly, this type of language is just confusing to me. Sure, it sounds good, very righteous, like many Sunday school answers, but does it really mean anything? What is "authentic" for a Christian? According to Paul, it is living "in the Spirit."

I have mentioned briefly in prior chapters the concept of partnering with God. At this point, with the necessary ground-work laid, I want to go into this idea in depth to present a picture of truly living "in the Spirit." For me, this is the central thrust of restoring Christianity to its original or earliest known state. In my opinion, this vital understanding is what has been lost through the centuries since Christ's resurrection. Just this week, I was describing to someone the idea of living each and every moment as a partner with God. As I finished with my descriptions and examples, she said, with wonder in her voice, "Why have I never heard about this before? I've never once heard a sermon preached on this. I don't hear other Christians talking like this. What happened?" I could not answer her question with certainty, but perhaps the reason is that few remember how to live this kind of life, and if I can't live it or understand it myself, I am surely not going to try to teach it.

I will begin with the way Jesus taught this concept to me. As I was praying, and asking Jesus to help me to better understand our relationship, He showed me this image:

I saw myself standing on the bottom of the ocean. I had no equipment at all. As I looked up, I saw the distance between me and the surface was so incredibly far, there was no way I could ever make it to the surface. Even if I were an Olympic swimmer I was dead already. There was no need to even try to start swimming; the distance determined the outcome.

In this way, Jesus revealed to me my true state without Him: dead already. As an interesting note, I know the reason Jesus chose this particular image for me. It was very personal, and made the point to me immediately. My husband is a scuba diving fan, and for years he has wanted me to get the training and certification so we could go diving together. He keeps claiming how much I would love seeing the underwater creation of God. My response has been uniformly the same: "There is too much water between me and the nearest air. No way!" Seeing myself standing on the ocean floor was the living experience of "one picture is worth a thousand words." I got it. I share this to point out an aspect of the partnership with God that I will explore further as we go along: He knows you intimately, He knows what has meaning to you, and He knows *how* to reach you and speak to you and bring you His truth in a very personal, very intimate way…in a way that *only* He knows. Do you see in this a reflection of how dependent we are on Him? To continue:

> Just then, Jesus was there on the ocean floor with me. Unlike me, He was fully equipped with all the necessary scuba gear (yes, it is OK to smile; Jesus in scuba gear *is* an "interesting" image). As only happens in the spiritual reality, I could hear His voice, even underwater through the regulator in his mouth. He said, "I will breathe you up."

For those of you not versed in scuba, this term is one employed if a diver runs out of oxygen in his or her tank, or has a catastrophic equipment failure, and another diver shares his or her regulator with the diver in trouble in order to get to the surface. The one diver's oxygen becomes the air for two. This is the reason for always having a "diving buddy."

> Jesus indicated that I was to hold onto Him, which I did. As we started up toward the surface, He would take the regulator out of His mouth and place it in mine. I began to notice that He would always do this before I was even aware that I was low on air or that I needed to take a breath; He anticipated my need before I knew I had it. I was not using my arms to swim, only to hold onto Him. He handled providing me with air and powering us together toward the surface.

Jesus used this part of the image to show me the meaning of partnership with Him. What was immediately clear to me was, if I *ever* let go of Him, even for a moment, I drown. The other understanding I received was a glimpse into how deeply Jesus loves me, and the strength that comes through that love and our being "one."

Several years later, I saw another image that reinforced the meaning of partnership, this time through a movie. However, if I had not received His initial expression of the relationship in that first image, the second would have held no personal meaning for my heart. As it was, I cried like a baby when I saw it, for I recognized it for what it was. The movie was *The Lord of the Rings: the Return of the King.* During the entire *Lord of the Rings* trilogy, Frodo and Sam had been on a quest together to destroy the power of evil in their world by returning the "one ring that rules them all" to the fires of Mount Doom. In this scene, they are climbing the mountain to reach the cave where they could finally, once and for all, destroy the ring. Frodo, carrying the weight of the ring, had lost all hope and collapsed under the ring's oppression. Sam sat next to Frodo, holding him, as fire and ash and impossible heat rained down around them, trying to help him remember the Shire, their home. Frodo, exhausted and consumed by the ring, could not recall a single taste or smell or sight of their home; all he could see was the lord of evil's eye looking into his very soul. At this, Sam, in tears, exclaims, "Let's be rid of it, then. I cannot carry it for you. But I can carry you!" He picks Frodo up onto his shoulders and begins to carry him the rest of the way up the mountain to destroy the ring. This image, so strikingly similar to the "carrying" of me that Jesus had originally shown me under the weight of the ocean, presents once again the relationship of true partners. One thing in that movie was certain: Sam loved Frodo more than he loved his own life. Doesn't that sound like Jesus?

To reiterate an important aspect of what Jesus taught me: *if I ever let go of Him, even for a moment, I drown.* So, living "in the Spirit" is a constant state of being. When I sleep at night, He guards my dreams. When I wake in the morning, His presence is my first experience. We talk in the grocery store, at the gas station, in Cody's hospital room...wherever I am, He is.

Most people, when I describe this "state of being," respond, "That sounds wonderful. Why don't I have that?" I offer two answers to that question (there may be more, but these are the two that Jesus has taught me to date that hinder His children): first, our expectations; second, our beliefs.

What do I mean by expectations? Several aspects of our expectations can get in our way. In fact, it was to address some of those expectations that we have written prior chapters. If I expect God to be uncaring, uninvolved, controlling, selfish, capricious, or callous, I am unlikely to expect Him to be there with me at all times wherever I am, nor am I likely to *want* Him to be there with me. Another expectation is simply not expecting a response from God. In this view, prayer looks like talking *at* God instead of sharing *with* God, and listening for His point of view is not something I am going to take the time to do if I don't even consider expecting a response. If I expect all of His "answers" to be the generalized truth in the Bible, I will not listen for personalized truth that addresses my intimate heart. On the other hand, if I expect His response to my prayer to be altering my circumstances, then my eyes will be on my external condition and not on His eyes. A difficult element is the question of whether I expect God to be real or not. This question reprises the earlier issue of knowing God as opposed to knowing *about* God. If I know about God only, I will most likely not expect Him to be an existent, actual part of my reality. If God is a concept to me, I will expect myself to live out His "concepts" in my own strength and ability. In addition to my expectations of God, then, another expectation is what I expect out of myself. Do I assume it is up to me? Do I suppose that I "should" be able to get it right? Do I see myself as on my own in life? One final expectation: do I expect this life to be too difficult, or even absolutely miserable, so I live in anticipation of finally reaching Heaven where at last I can know some peace? Or do I expect peace *now*?

Let's look now at some beliefs that can hinder a partnering relationship with God. For this discussion, I refer to the truth found in story of the fall of man as portrayed in Genesis 3. Three beliefs stand out in this tale: the first, and most problematic, is the belief that I can be like God. I call this belief the "self" lie. It undergirds all other false beliefs we have, and is the root of all of our problems. Consider this aspect of the belief: if I see myself as my own "god," why would I choose to partner with another God? On the contrary, I would not want to partner with anyone or anything, so that I could continue to see myself as the god-center of my universe. Accepting the "self" lie led to the knowledge of good and evil being in us. From it, I know sin, and from sin I know death. There are two sides to the self-lie coin: "heads" is the one most easily recognizable, which is pride. These beliefs sound like, "I'm better than," "I'm more important than," and "I, me, mine" statements of all types. "Tails," often ignored or misrepresented as humility, and often reinforced by the church, sounds like "I am unimportant," "I am worthless," "I'll never be good enough," and other similar self-debasing statements. What I want you to notice, however, is that they are still "I" statements, and they still reflect a view of self as the center of all things: a worthless center, but a center nonetheless. "I am above all" and "I am nothing" are actually the same belief reflected on two extremes; both have to do with self as "god."

In the Genesis story, two other beliefs grow out of the original "sin" of self. They are stated in verse 10: "I heard you in the garden and I was afraid...I was naked so I hid." These two beliefs, fear and shame, are the results or consequences of the acceptance of myself as my own god. First, as related in this story, my "eyes will be opened" to my own nakedness, and I immediately try to cover it up. Shame, then, is covering up or hiding, and thereby separating myself from God. A huge amount of our personal energy is spent in trying to cover ourselves up. One example of our hiding is our tendency to pretend with others, and before God. This inclination is so strong in us that we have adopted beliefs directing us to pretend and justifying it as righteousness, such as "act like you are supposed to, not how you feel," and "ignore your feelings for they are deceitful." I will go into these types of beliefs further in the next chapter.

Another response to shame within us is to disconnect from others; in other words, to build up a wall of self-protection (see the presence of fear showing up also?) within our hearts that we hide behind. We eschew vulnerability in favor of an illusion of control (pretending again we can prevent hurt and ignoring the fact that it still hurts even behind our wall, but choosing to believe the illusion anyway). As a result, we cannot have true relationships, nor can we follow the primary commandments of Jesus and the law: to love God with all our hearts, and to love our neighbor as we love ourselves. There are many examples of hiding in shame, but I will only address one more. I have alluded before to how Satan's lies create the opposite of our desired goals, and lead us 180 degrees from God's truth. Shame tells us that we must "prepare" ourselves to come before God. If I can get it right, do it right, make myself clean, then and only then can I come into His presence. So I hide from Him, and start the effort toward self-cleaning. In truth, the only cleansing of my sin comes through the Holy Spirit's work in my heart, as the many verses we have quoted from Paul's writings in this chapter indicate. So hiding myself from Him and refusing to come into His presence until I think I'm "ready" and "good enough" keeps me from ever reaching the very thing I am trying to accomplish. Another enemy Catch-22.

Shame beliefs sound like "should" and "shouldn't" statements, blaming and fault finding statements, and seeing myself as "bad." The church seems to have a lot of confusion regarding the difference between shame and guilt. In fact, the two words are often used interchangeably. In order to clarify this for you, I will simply say that shame is a "bad me" belief while guilt is the recognition of a bad choice. Guilt is motivating me to make a different choice next time, while shame is condemning of my nature. As you think on this difference, remember Paul's teaching that the old is gone, and the new has come. Jesus' payment for my sin has left me free from condemnation, as stated in Romans 8:1. Guilt, therefore, is a true belief (I can make a bad choice, and often do) while shame is a lie belief (because there is no condemnation).

The second belief, fear, is shame's "partner." In my counseling practice, the single most prevalent symptom that motivates people to seek counseling is fear. The vast majority of people make most of their significant decisions out of fear. For example, I am afraid of being alone, so I settle for someone whom I think is "good enough," but whom I do not really love. This results in an unhappy marriage, which emotionally and/or physically leaves me alone. I am afraid my children will hate me, so I don't act as a parent; I try to behave as a friend. Of course, as a result, when they reach teenage years, they hate me. On the other end of that issue, I am afraid my children will do something stupid, so I exert extreme control over them or I try to protect them from exposure to any "bad" thing. They respond (again during adolescence) by rebelling and doing the opposite of what I tried to force them into doing. I hate my job but I am too afraid to try to find another one, fearing it might be worse, so I leave myself as miserable as I am afraid I would be somewhere else. I could go on (and on), but I want to point out the outcome in each example, which reflects a truth from God: *we always create what we most fear*. Write that one down, because it is extremely important, and test it in your own life. You will see example after example of making decisions based on fear leading you down the wrong path. Just as in the midst of shame I end up 180 degrees from where God is and what He desires for me, when I decide out of fear, I walk 180 degrees from where I intended to go, and I walk away from God. Fear beliefs include "I have to but I can't," "doom is around the corner," "I am powerless and trapped," and similar statements.

The self beliefs, fear beliefs, and shame beliefs all result in the same consequence: separation from God. That perceived distance from Him, imposed by my beliefs, *not by Him*, directly impedes my ability to communicate, to relate to, and to have intimacy with God. Do you see how, believing I am my own god, I would not ask God for direction and help? Do you see how, in hiding myself and trying to save myself, I cut off the presence of the One Who can save me? Do you see how choosing based on a motivation of fear prevents a motivation of love, of relationship, or of God's desires to be with me?

So what can I do about this mess? I have just presented how and why we cannot change this problem of "sin" within ourselves. So is it hopeless? If I can't do it, what can possibly help me? Ummm, wrong question. Can you recognize now, based on this discussion, the error in this question? What lies are present in it? (All three are represented, if you will look beyond the surface).

It all goes back to the centerpiece of our lives: knowing Who God really is. Recognition is the first and most important piece of this process of coming to the answers to that fundamental question. In part, this book has been about recognition: trying to point out the things that hinder us from intimacy with God, so that we can recognize those beliefs and bring them to God for His help in removing them and replacing them in our hearts with His truth. For example, if I have always believed that God is distant from me, I will never think to question if this is true. The same goes for the myriad other perceptions we have discussed in previous chapters. If those beliefs have been taught to us and reinforced in us, we won't realize the need to challenge them.

My role in the partnership is to hold onto Jesus. Remember the image under water? If I recognize my state without Him (I am dead already) and I am willing to receive His offered help, each problem area in my heart (I have no equipment, I am too far from the surface to make it, I can't swim fast enough or well enough to save myself, I am running out of air, I have no other resource) can be addressed; not by my efforts, but by His interventions. He has an answer for each hindrance within me. The real question is: Am I willing to hold onto Him, face to face and second by second, and allow Him to provide what I need?

Chapter 10

Transformation

The Current State of the Church and External Focus for a Changed Life

Week after week in my counseling practice, I listen to people who have come to my office for "help," asking what they have to "do" to be better. I suppose they have read the self-help books and are looking for me to give them a new, more effective "list of six." Maybe they have heard sermons that outlined the steps they had to follow or the things they had to do to be good Christians, and they assume I also have steps or an outline. (A horrid image of me handing my clients a fill-in-the-blank outline form, as used in so many churches today, and sitting in my chair prompting them to guess the right word to put in the blank spaces just flew into my mind). Perhaps they are seeking a "quick fix" or a tangible skill or behavior that if they can just "put it on" or "act as if" it will solve their problems.

A long time ago, I actually had a small wooden "magic wand" with a painted yellow star at the top, a leftover from my days working with children and their families, that I pulled out as a reminder to my clients that there was no such thing as magic. I would suggest they wave it over themselves or bonk themselves in the head with it, and see if it changed them (most of them got my point without trying the exercise). Today, I simply ask a question: "Do you believe Jesus would want you to pretend you are changed?"

It is surprising that most individuals do not consider "putting on" a behavior as pretending; however, the popular religious adage "fake it 'til you make it" reveals more clearly the supposition that I am supposed to pretend until I finally get it "right" and don't have to pretend anymore. However, pretending is tantamount to lying, and I question if lying will ever be a path to "get it right." Lying would certainly not be God's path toward change.

Cognitive-behavioral psychologists believe in a theory that states if you change your thinking, you will change both the behavioral response and the emotion engendered by a stimulus. This process looks like feeling a feeling in response to some event in my life, stopping myself and purposefully altering my thinking about the event, then behaving as if I don't feel the way I felt about the event anymore, then repeating the steps each time I feel that feeling again, ad infinitum. As an example, I make a mistake; in response, I feel stupid; I tell myself I am not stupid and everyone makes mistakes; then I move on until I make another mistake and feel stupid again. I have noted two things about this theory: first, that it might appear to work for that one event, if and when I recognize my own thinking or belief about the stimulus event, but the change does not extend to all other situations that stir up those feelings in me. Second, that when I am under stress, I immediately return to what I call "my baseline," which is my emotional response based on my strongest and earliest learned beliefs, no matter what I try to tell myself to believe. Put simply, this stepwise process doesn't *change* me.

Along a parallel line of thinking as employed by cognitive behaviorists, I also hear church members focusing on the deceitfulness of the heart, saying, "Don't trust your emotions; they will mislead you." I want to ask, "What are you saying, that the mind *doesn't* deceive us? That I am to rely on my own thinking as trustworthy but know my own heart as a liar?" We have just completed a chapter talking about intimacy, oneness and partnership with God as an internal state of being, something that occurs in the heart. If this relationship occurs in the heart, and the heart cannot be trusted, how can we trust our partnership with God? And if I am "faking" my behavior to mimic "righteousness," is not my behavior also deceitful, like my heart and my mind?

I believe some will consider these suggestions dangerous; similarly, people in Paul's time considered some of his ideas dangerous and drew false assumptions from them that he wrote letters to dispute. Am I saying it doesn't matter what we do, that behavior is unimportant, so we should go ahead and do whatever we want? As we have stated previously, if you go from one extreme to the other on the same plane, you merely jump to the other side of the same lie: the only question then is, heads or tails? Am I saying we are powerless and trapped by our beliefs and emotions, and therefore can do nothing, so we should just give up and give in? The last chapter identified for you this type of language as reflecting fear and shame beliefs, based therefore in the sin nature. Am I stating that we have no accountability for our choices; that we have freedom given from God but no responsibility? These questions are not far afield from statements made in Paul's time in response to his teaching.

Historical Analysis

Paul's letters contain many descriptions about behaviors, and what behaviors he considered to be appropriate for followers of Christ. Does this mean that the early churches were held to a list of "Christian" actions that would make them better in God's eyes? As we have already seen, Paul argues on many occasions that righteousness cannot be gained through the law (his example for "works" or behaviors). However, if Paul believes that behavior, "works", cannot gain righteousness, then why does he urge his churches to behave in certain ways? The answer to this question can be found in a response that Paul gives to a hypothetical question similar to one posed in the first section of this chapter:

> Shall we sin because we are not under the law but under grace? (Romans 6:15)

In other words, can followers of Christ behave any way they want because they are not held to any standard of the "law" (system of behaviors or works), but are saved by belief in the gospel? Paul answers:

> By no means! Don't you know that when you offer yourselves to someone to obey him as slaves, you are slaves to the one whom you obey – whether you are slaves to sin, which leads to death, or to obedience, which leads to righteousness? (Romans 6:15-16)

What is important to note here is that Paul begins first with submission to God, and ends with behavior. The actions are resultant, not causative. When one offers oneself up for slavery to God (recalling the discussion of slavery as freedom), the result is that this obedience (dependence) leads to righteousness. Keeping in mind again that, in Paul's theology, there is no system of behaviors (law) that can lead to righteousness, his answer is that dependence comes first and leads to the resultant behavior. Thus, Paul can chastise the churches for engaging in behaviors he considered "sin" because, "We died to sin (by dying with Jesus through the belief that Jesus died and was resurrected as payment for sin); how can we live in it any longer (Romans 6:2)?"

Examining I Corinthians reinforces the contention that Paul believes in freedom and choice, rather than lists of behaviors. Paul writes the church at Corinth that, "It is actually reported that there is sexual immorality among you, and of a kind that does not occur even among pagans...And you are proud! (I Corinthians 5:1)." This shocked accusation may, on the surface, appear to contradict the argument presented in this chapter, except that Paul states several times the apparent boast of the Corinthian church, that, "Everything is permissible for me (I Corinthians 6:12; 10:23)." This statement is a belief with which Paul does not disagree, and may have even been something he personally taught the church (especially if the members were quoting the statement as justification for their behaviors, as they seem to be). Notice that he does not negate the statement; he does not say in response, "No, you are wrong, not everything is permissible." Rather, he couples the declaration with qualifiers; "Everything is permissible for me' – but not everything is beneficial (6:12 and 10:23); but I will not be mastered by anything (6:12); but not everything is constructive (10:23)."

The letter to Corinth provides a concrete example of the problem Paul addresses at Rome: that people misunderstood Paul's teaching and believed they could do anything because they were no longer under the law. Paul did believe that everything was permissible because he was no longer under the law, but this was not encouragement to participate in everything. Instead, as shown by his statement to the Roman church, Paul assumes that people who believed the gospel and had "died to sin," would then choose on their own to practice beneficial, constructive behaviors, and not to engage in any activity simply because they could. There was no list of "condemned" and "righteous" behaviors, but there are constructive, beneficial behaviors that are in line with what the church professed to believe. However, Paul only applied these statements to those claiming to be believers. Thus, he makes a distinction between those who are inside and outside the church:

> I have written to you in my letter not to associate with sexually immoral people – not at all meaning the people of this world who are immoral, or the greedy and swindlers, or idolaters. In that case you would have to leave this world. But now I am writing you that you must not associate with anyone *who calls himself a brother* but is sexually immoral or greedy, an idolater or a slanderer, a drunkard or a swindler... What business is it of mine to judge those *outside the church?* (I Corinthians 5:9-12, italics added for emphasis)

Notice here that, by making the distinction between believers and non-believers, Paul makes being a "brother" a requirement that has to come first, before any of the behavioral changes are to be expected (not just relating to sexual immorality, because he includes a long list of other behaviors as well). Belief comes first, behavior second.

Paul also specifically refers to Christian participation in the communal sacrificial meals at Corinth. In Greco-Roman cities, religion was a public affair, and a large part of involvement in the civic religion was participation in the public sacrifices.

This mainly consisted of observing as a crowd, while the priests performed the rituals and sacrifice, and then sharing in a meal cooked from the sacrifice. Neglecting to attend these sacrifices was frowned upon by the community, as the sacrifices were intended for the benefit of the entire populace, to ensure the prosperity of the town, and to gain the protection of the gods. In addition to the religious function served by the sacrifice, the rituals were also an important group social gathering, (like church services today, which serve a larger social function than simply sitting, passively watching the rituals and listening to the message). This communal aspect not only allowed for the shared experience of the religious ritual, but also for the latest news and information to be passed along (you still never hear more gossip than when you are in a church service). The public rituals also served an even greater purpose, one that might not immediately register with members of today's surplus society: the meat from the sacrifices often provided people with their only source of dietary protein.[25] Paul's letter to Corinth hints that people were still attending these public sacrifices, and that certain members of the church were condemning those who ate the meat sacrificed to the pagan "idols." In response, Paul explains:

> So, then, about food sacrificed to idols: We know that an idol is nothing at all in the world and that there is no God but one... But not everyone knows this. Some people are still so accustomed to idols that when they eat such food they think of it as having been sacrificed to an idol, and since their conscience is weak, it is defiled. But food does not bring us near to God; we are no worse if we do not eat, and no better if we do. (I Corinthians 8:4-8).

Just as he does with the statement that "everything is permissible," Paul couples this statement that all food is permissible with a qualifier:

> Be careful, however, that the exercise of your freedom does not become a stumbling block to the weak. For if anyone with a weak conscience sees you who have this knowledge eating in an idol's temple, won't he be emboldened to eat what has been sacrificed to idols? So this weak brother, for whom Christ died, is destroyed by your knowledge (because he does not believe that all foods are clean, but eats simply because he witnessed another's behavior)… Therefore, if what I eat causes my brother to fall into sin, I will never eat meat again, so that I will not cause him to fall. (I Corinthians 8:9-13, parenthetical material added)

A similar situation seemed to be happening at Rome. Paul explains at length how people had been judging members of the Christian community who were engaging in "disputable" behaviors:

> Accept him whose faith is weak, without passing judgment on disputable matters. One man's faith allows him to eat everything, but another man, whose faith is weak, eats only vegetables. The man who eats everything must not look down on him who does not, and the man who does not eat everything must not condemn the man who does, for God has accepted him. Who are you to judge another man's servant? …One man considers one day more sacred than another; another man considers every day alike. Each one should be fully convinced in his own mind. He who regards one day as special, does so to the Lord. He who eats meat, eats to the Lord, for

he gives thanks to God; and he who abstains, does so to the Lord and gives thanks to God... Therefore, let us stop passing judgment on one another. Instead, make up your mind not to put any stumbling block or obstacle in your brother's way. As one who is in the Lord Jesus, I am fully convinced that no food [or, 'that nothing'] is unclean in itself... If your brother is distressed by what you eat, you are no longer acting in love. Do not by your eating destroy your brother for whom Christ died... Let us therefore make every effort to do what leads to peace and to mutual edification... All food is clean, but it is wrong for a man to eat anything that causes someone else to stumble. (Romans 14:1-20)

This lengthy passage makes it clear that for Paul, "the kingdom of God is not a matter of eating or drinking (behaviors), but of righteousness, peace and joy in the Holy Spirit (Romans 15:17)." As sin is the condition of alienation rather than specific behaviors, so is righteousness the condition of relationship. To Paul, even though all behaviors are now "allowed" because of his freedom, this does not mean that they are productive or in line with the belief "we died to sin." Thus, Paul does not believe that behaviors in and of themselves cause uncleanness, but that motivation from the heart is what results in "sin" behaviors. Additionally, if motivated by love (the law and the commandments, Romans 13:9) and one's freedom (through slavery to God), then one freely decides to act out of love; resolving to edify, and not to hinder another, who may not see freedom in behavior in quite so free a way, even if this means abstaining from certain activities (in which they may be free to participate and do not in themselves provide any condemnation). Thus, Paul uses his freedom to freely decide to give up his freedom:

Though I am free and belong to no man, I make myself a slave to everyone... To the Jews I became like a Jew, to win the Jews. To those under the law I became like one under the law (though I myself am not under the law), so as to win those under the law. To those not having the law I became like one not having the law (though I am not free from God's law but am under Christ's law), so as to win those not having the law. To the weak I became weak, to win the weak. I have become all things to all men so that by all possible means I might save some. (I Corinthians 9:19-22)

Restored State of the Transformational Power of the Truth

If changing behavior does not bring about internalized transformation, then what does? According to Paul, it is the presence of the Holy Spirit:

Now the Lord is the Spirit, and where the Spirit of the Lord is, there is freedom. And we, who with unveiled faces all reflect the Lord's glory, are being transformed into His likeness with ever-increasing glory, which comes from the Lord, who is the Spirit. (II Corinthians 3:18).

Thus we are "transformed" by the presence of the Holy Spirit. "Being transformed with ever-increasing glory" seems to indicate a process of change that occurs in us rather than an instantaneous or momentary jolt of difference. However, there seems to be little talk in today's church about that internal change process, with most of the focus of sermons and teaching being about changing behavior. Changing behaviors may seem easier or more clear and straightforward to us, based on our belief (however false or delusional) that we can "control" the behavioral aspects of our lives, as opposed to a change of heart, which seems conceptual and illusory. Nevertheless, pasting lemons onto an orange tree does not make the orange tree a lemon tree. It might look rather lemony for a time, but those lemons will fall off and the tree is still the same orange tree at its root. As noted, with behaviors and cognitions, stress or difficulty sends us reeling back to "baseline." If "baseline" in our hearts is not changed, ultimately we are not "transformed."

My experiences with clients seeking change in their lives who have partnered with Christ to reach those changes have shown some consistent elements. First and foremost, two truths appear to be absolutely crucial to internal change: the first is knowing Who God really is, and the second is knowing who He says we are. But how do we discover these truths for ourselves?

It might be nice (again that perception of ease) for us to think we can read the Bible and know the truths from that study. What we can receive from the Bible is the possibility of knowing the truth *cognitively* (in other words, with head-knowledge). What does not happen, however, is transformation of the heart (heart-knowledge). Unfortunately, what results for us from gaining head-knowledge but still having a lack of truth at the heart-level is an internal division, an ongoing self-argument within us that destroys any peace we may have and ultimately tries to destroy us. Here is an example of what I am talking about: I can look on the wall of my office and see the multiple degrees, including my rather large and very nicely framed Ph.D. I can count the awards and recognitions I have received over the years. I can look around and see that I own my own successful business. I can look at my three children and see three incredible individuals who have grown into amazing human beings in all areas of their lives, which I could believe reflects well on me. I can look at my 28-year marriage as a testament to our wonderful relationship, of which I am a part. Seeing all of these wonderful things in my life, I can say to myself, "I have value," and that feels good…for the moment. None of these things will matter at all to me, however, if I believe in my heart that I am worthless. Instead, if someone responds to me negatively, as if I am worthless or valueless or meaningless, I will feel worthless and valueless and meaningless because those things feel true in my heart. I will not stop to think about the many wonderful things I have listed in my mind, because my heart will be screaming the lies at me. It is true that, if I recognize what is going on, I can stop my response to the negative feedback and list again for myself all the wonderful things in my life. This exercise may change the feeling response in that moment, but it still creates an internal argument. What if the feedback is from a significant individual in my life, though? What if I do something that causes terrible results or consequences for my family, significant others, or myself? At that point, the beliefs in my heart will feel very true, reinforced by my circumstances, and no cognitive exercise is going to impact those feelings. Using this example, do you see how it is possible for me to say I am valuable based on the things I have identified for myself as measures of my worth, while at the very same time feeling as if I am worthless? That is the internal division I am describing.

Jesus used a true story in my life as a symbol to teach me some things about internal change. When the builders cleared the land for our home, they cut down one tree that was situated very near to the house's foundation. They proceeded to cut the stump down until it was below ground level and covered it with dirt. After we moved in, however, we noticed what appeared to be a young tree growing up out of the ground near the side of our house. When we checked it out, we found that the branches were growing out of the covered-over stump. That was in 1992. The tree, completely renewed, now stands taller than the roof of our two-story house. It is full and leafy and quite healthy, as evidenced by our clogged gutters in the fall. Jesus spoke to me about this tree, and pointed out that the builders had cut down the tree, pruned out the branches, even covered over the remains, but they did not remove the root. As a result, the tree grew back. This process, He said, mirrors the process in us when we try to cognitively "control" our feelings instead of removing the root causes of our problems. Those root issues have been identified in the previous chapter, the results of the presence of sin in the world: self, fear, and shame.

Why is it that I cannot change my own root beliefs? The answer is found in the word "authority." Someone who speaks with authority speaks with certainty, as an expert, someone totally versed in all knowledge with evidence of that knowledge in the area in question. For example, an art historian is an expert in that field. You would not consult an electrician on a question of the authenticity of a piece of artwork. The electrician might have an opinion, as in "it looks good to me," but he or she does not speak with authority. The art historian, if properly credentialed, does. He or she knows exactly how to evaluate the artwork for authenticity and can spot a forgery, because he or she is an expert.

Interestingly, we are not "experts" about ourselves. Many things about ourselves are hidden from us, such as unconscious motivations and processes. People in "authority" over us have influenced our beliefs about ourselves since we were born, and we are not able to speak with absolute certainty about our own natures, nor are we able to separate the truth from the fiction accurately. Because we are unable to speak with "authority" to our own hearts, we are unable to change our own beliefs at the heart-level. Only the Holy Spirit, Who created us and is *the* authority on us, Who knows everything about us on every level, even on the unconscious level, can transform our hearts. What changes us is God's truth, spoken to us with authority by the Holy Spirit within us. Only then can we be certain, because *the* authority on us has told us.

The key word in the transformation process is **listening**. However, I cannot listen to a voice that is not present within me. Thus, before there can be behavior change, there must first be belief. I must receive the gift of the presence of the Holy Spirit in my heart before I can listen to His words of truth spoken in my heart. No amount of effort on my part to make behavioral changes is going to create a "Holy-Spirit equivalent" in me.

After belief comes the "getting to know" phase of relationship. He shares Himself with me, and I share myself with Him. We could say this parallels "dating" before you move toward "marriage." This is a time of constant companionship, partnering together in all things, getting used to and expecting Him to always be there, and, most importantly, finding out about His nature. You learn from Him Who He is, and what you can expect from Him. You see and experience what He is like in various situations with you. Your trust in Him grows and expands with each experience of His love for you.

The next phase of relationship is the "marriage;" the internal transformation period. As your intimacy and relationship grows, you become "one." "But he who unites himself with the Lord is one with Him in spirit (I Corinthians 6:17)." He begins to point out to you the beliefs that cause you pain, those that are opposed to Him and His truth, and because your trust in Him has grown, you can receive what He is showing you and telling you. Self beliefs, shame beliefs, and fear beliefs are exposed for what they are. What has felt true to you, and you have not questioned about yourself to that point, He helps you to explore. During this time, following your knowledge of Who He is, He is able to share with you who you are, based on who He created you to be. He also reveals to your heart the truths that replace the self, fear, and shame beliefs. Through this process, your heart is made new.

Following the internal transformation comes the behavioral change. Finally, right? I can imagine the reader breathing a sigh of relief that at last they are going to *do* something. Wrong. This is the last part of the change process to occur. However, there is a critical point here: *the behavior change of which I speak is not done with your effort.* This phase of the process is also a state of being. Remember, belief, getting to know, and intimate internal transformation must all come first, and our behavior alters as a natural outgrowth of those other transformation processes. In other words, if my heart believes differently from the past and knows the truth of God, I will behave differently out of that new belief. The new behaviors will flow from me quite naturally. Additionally, I *want* to behave differently, because I have experienced the unequalled love of Jesus for *me* and the desire of my heart is to love Him in return. The truth becomes my air, water, food, and rest. Do you recall the brief discussion earlier of Maslow's hierarchy of needs? What happens in my heart is that the truth becomes the primary level of my hierarchy, the basic survival level. His presence is the one thing I cannot do without.

So, first I meet Jesus; I am there (state of being verb) and He introduces Himself to me. Then we spend time being together (state of being verb), getting acquainted, sharing experiences and learning about each other. Finally, as intimacy grows through being one in spirit (state of being verb), He shares His truth with me and transforms my heart's beliefs in the process, which in turn changes my behavior. Trying to change behaviors in order to transform the heart is like trying to pick an orange off of an orange tree before the seed has been planted. It just doesn't work that way.

I remember "meeting Jesus" when I was 13 years old. A friend had invited me to a revival service at her church geared to the youth, and as they talked about Jesus, I consciously thought, "I have met Him before." Now I know this may not make much sense to you, for I was not raised in a Christian home, but it was crystal clear to me that night, and since that night, that this new "meeting" was actually a reminder of Jesus' initiative in introducing Himself to me at some earlier point in my life. I *recognized* Him and I believed He was my Savior that night.

I also remember when Jesus told me about who I am, who He created me to be. This occurred many years later, after I had discovered a newfound intimacy with Him and began to learn to listen to Him and trust Him. He showed me an image of a steep cliff overlooking an angry ocean; a storm was raging and it was night. Standing on the cliff's edge was a tall, Viking-like woman, complete with metal cone-shaped hat with horns curving off of each side, dressed in battle regalia, and two long braids trailing from under the helmet. The Viking woman had a huge sword, which she pointed out toward the ocean, and she issued a challenge to enemy warships to come ashore to face her, for she was ready. She was strong and confident, and she clearly loved a good fight. He called her, "Helga." Now think about it; if I was going to choose a name or an image for the Lord to give me, it wouldn't have been "Helga" or a Viking warrior. Wouldn't something sweet and gentle, kind of a "Bambi" image, have been more attractive…and Christ-like? Yet, when I saw this image, I knew immediately in my heart it was my true self, and it was the truth of me. And years later, here I am, Helga-ing my way through this very writing, fighting a pitched battle against the enemy's deception of God's church.

He also gave me another name: Anna. This name came from a scene He picked from the old musical, *The King and I*. In the scene, the King (Yul Brynner) and Anna (Deborah Kerr) are celebrating a tremendous success where the King had hosted dinner for a British envoy. As they talk and share their excitement following the dinner, the King asks Anna about seeing her dancing with one of the British guests. As they do in musicals from that era, she breaks into song. This is the point in the scene where Jesus started my image for me. If you are familiar with this movie, you know that this scene is loud and fast, high-energy and full of deep passion. In my image, instead of Yul Brynner, there Jesus was, dressed in the Kingly Siamese silks…and there I stood, dressed in a beautiful ball gown, with hoop skirts, just like Anna. Jesus, strong and authoritative like a King, reached His arms out toward me, and we began to dance; just as in the musical, we whirled with reckless abandon around and around the floor. I have never felt such complete joy. When the music ended, He and I stood across from each other, panting, and He stared at me with an intensity, passion, intimacy and love unmatched in my life experience. Then, as in the movie, He thrust His hand out to me and said, "Again." The music cranked back up, and we were once more flying across the floor together, one in movement and filled with the plea-sure of the moment. So, He told me, I am His Warrior and I am His beautiful and much-adored Dance Partner…Helga Anna.

I believe we each have a unique identity, a "name" if you will, since for the Jewish people of Jesus' time, a name and identity were synonymous. I also believe that, once we know Him, and by this I mean truly know His nature and what to expect from Him, and feel the depth of His love for us, He can show us our actual identities, our true names. We will recognize ourselves, and remember who He made us to be. Out of that truth flows behavior that matches that knowledge. As I said, Jesus and I dance our way as partners through each day, and I "Helga" my way through counseling, through teaching, and through the writing of this book. I can do nothing else, for it is who I am. My behavior matches the Spirit-transformed heart within me, but that heart-level, internal change must occur first, or no lasting behavior change will follow.

Chapter 11

Purpose

The Current State of the Church and the Purpose-Driven Mentality

"It isn't about you."[26] This statement can be found in many currently popular Christian books and heard ringing from pulpits and in Bible study materials. Recently, I even saw it blazoned across the front of a t-shirt in a Christian gift catalog. It is presented without examination or question, as absolute fact. We are told to seek God's purpose for us, and this task is defined as figuring out what God wants us to do within the context of His greater agenda to further the Plan. Additionally, everything that happens furthers that agenda, no matter what form or effect the circumstances take or have. My importance to God is completely defined by my purpose in the Plan. Mainly, since I am simply a tiny part of the overall progression of God's agenda, the Plan is the only thing. I do not matter, beyond my miniscule contribution to the furthering of the Plan. But I am so grateful to be a part of the Master Plan, even if just as a nondescript and unnoticed "hair on the flea on the bump on the log in the hole at the bottom of the sea," I am willing to view myself through the lens of that contribution alone. I become my "purpose." The "I" that I am ceases to exist, or at best is rendered completely irrelevant.

That's not all! I am told, in the framework of my "purpose-driven mentality," that this attitude is spiritual maturity. I am assured that my self-debasement is really humility, and that anything else would be "pride," and therefore sin (not just any sin but a terrible sin, one of the worst). I am shown individual verses in the Bible and told they indicate that I must cease to exist, I am not important, and only the Plan matters to God. Pain and personal misery further the Plan; giving up on my greatest dream furthers the Plan; making cinnamon rolls for church visitors furthers the Plan, even if I can't cook at all. Whatever it is, if it happens or is "asked" of me, it furthers the Plan. If my child dies to further the Plan, so be it; I should be thankful he died for he has fulfilled his "purpose." To believe anything else is to be selfish. I am sacrificed on the altar to the "greater" purpose.

I am also told that this greater purpose, this God-agenda, demonstrates the vast majesty and power of God. We are instructed to see His sovereignty, His glory, His wonder, His awesomeness, and even His love, all reflected in how He progresses the Plan. Somehow, if I don't focus on God's "agenda," I will miss seeing His greatness, as if His majesty will be diminished in my eyes. I suppose that if it is God's Plan, it has to be *big*. Perhaps if I perceive the complexity, magnificence and colossal extension throughout existence and time of God's Master Plan, I will capture a fragment, a tiny glimpse of Who God is.

It isn't about me. "It" is about the Plan.

But I have to ask: if it isn't about me, and wasn't ever about me, and will never be about me, why did Jesus die on the cross....*for me?*

Historical Analysis

Was Paul a proponent of the belief that humans are insignificant and do not matter to God? We can start the path to answering this question with Paul's own words:

> God demonstrates his own love for us in this: while we
> were still sinners, Christ died for us. (Romans 5:8)

This quote reveals three firm beliefs held by Paul: God loves us; God loved us even though we were "ungodly;" and because God loves us, Christ died. We already know that Paul firmly believed that Jesus died and was raised by God in order to save mankind (I Corinthians 15:3-8; Romans 8:3-4; Galatians 4:4-5). This is Paul's gospel; this is the hinge point of his faith: "if Christ has not been raised, our preaching is useless and so is your faith (I Corinthians 15:14)." We also already know that Paul considered Jesus to be God's Son ("He who did not spare his own Son" (Romans 8:31)), and even "in very nature God" (Romans 8:3-4; Philippians 2:6). Thus, Paul is stating that God loved humanity such that he would send his Son to die to redeem us (In other words, John 3:16). For Paul, God thought mankind important enough to redeem: "He who did not spare his own Son, but gave him up for us all (Romans 8:31)."

Another statement by Paul can help further illuminate his beliefs:

> And we know that in all things God works for the good
> of those who love him, who have been called according
> to his purpose. (Romans 8:28)

Notice here that Paul explains it as God working for those who love him and not vice versa. This verse does not state, "And we know that in all things those who love God work for the good of him..." We have already discussed works, and what Paul thought about the idea of earning salvation. For Paul, behaviors come secondary, out of the response of love. Therefore, those who love God reflect that love, and he works for their good because he loves them. Additionally, the second half of this verse poses an important question: What is God's purpose, his Master Plan, if you will?

Paul answers this question immediately. In Romans 8:29-30, he explains God's purpose for us: "to be conformed to the likeness of his Son, that he (the Son) might be the firstborn among many brothers." For Paul, God's Plan revolves around mankind. His purpose is conforming those who love him to the likeness of Jesus. In this conformation, people are elevated to the status of siblings with Jesus. Would siblingship with God's Son make humanity children of God as well? Paul firmly believes so, and more:

> Because you are sons, God sent the Spirit of his Son into our hearts, the Spirit who calls out, 'Abba, Father.' So you are no longer a slave, but a son; and since you are a son, God has made you also an heir. (Galatians 4:6-7)

Paul goes as far as to claim, not only that God found us important enough to not spare his own Son, but that we are significant enough to him to make us his children, as well as heirs to his kingdom. "You are no longer a slave (to sin);" you are a slave to God, and he has elevated you to equal status with Jesus. You are no longer insignificant and on the lowest rung of the totem pole. Instead, Paul firmly believes that we have value enough to be heirs of God. Paul makes this exact same claim to the Roman church as well:

> For you did not receive a spirit that makes you a slave again to fear, but a Spirit of sonship. And by him we cry, 'Abba, father.' The Spirit himself testifies that we are

God's children. Now if we are children, then we are heirs – heirs of God and co-heirs with Christ...(Romans 8:15-17)

Notice in both examples that Paul places the onus again on God. It is through the Spirit of God and Jesus that we become children and heirs. This same Spirit is the one we have already discussed multiple times in previous chapters. Again, Paul believes firmly that receiving righteousness, the Spirit, and status as children and heirs is dependent upon nothing we do. Paul states clearly:

This righteousness from God comes through faith in Jesus Christ...for all have sinned and fall short of the glory of God, and are justified *freely* by his grace that came through the redemption that came by Christ Jesus (Romans 3:22-24, italics added)

Enumerating an example of this, Paul explains:

Now when a man works, his wages are not credited to him as a gift, but as an obligation. However, to the man who does not work but trusts God who justifies the wicked, his faith is credited to him as righteousness (And the righteousness is a gift, since the man does not work, but trusts God). (Romans 4:4-5)

Tying together everything we have studied so far, Paul believed that God valued humanity such that, in order to place them in the position of his children and heirs, he sent Jesus, his Son, to die in their stead. Humanity, in turn, did nothing to deserve this, but was given redemption through grace, so that whoever believes God will be given the free gifts of righteousness and the Spirit. These gifts are not based on any of their own efforts, because if they were, the gifts would cease to be gifts and become a wage and obligation. Those who believe God did this will respond with love, becoming slaves to God, because God loved them first. Thus God will fulfill his purpose for them, which is conforming them to the likeness of Jesus, with whom they are now equal in status, value, importance, significance, and worth.

If God's purpose for humanity is that we be conformed to the likeness of Jesus, what does this look like? In other words, what is the likeness of Jesus? Paul answers this question as well:

> Your attitude should be the same as that of Christ Jesus: Who, being in very nature God, did not consider equality with God something to be grasped, but made himself nothing, taking the very nature of a servant... he humbled himself and became obedient to death... (Philippians 2:5-8)

For Paul, conformation to the likeness of Jesus is becoming a servant. This is the nature of humility for Paul, and fits well with his belief that slavery to God is freedom. We discussed in a previous chapter Paul's belief in the two-sided coin of freedom and slavery. Slavery to God, then, results in elevation to the status of children and co-heirs. As we have already seen, Paul used his freedom to give up his freedom to become "all things to all people." Thus Paul, being confident in his freedom and position as a son of God, a brother to Christ, and an heir to the kingdom, could joyfully present himself for any type of servitude in any circumstances. This is the same declaration he makes about Jesus. He explains that Jesus, certain of his standing as an equal to God, was then able to relinquish his freedom and become a humble servant, even to his death. Thus, Paul models in his own actions his description of the likeness of Jesus, evidence of his claim that he is conformed to the likeness of Christ. This attitude of love and servitude, while being certain of his true status, is humility according to Paul.

Restored State of Relationship-focused Mentality

I matter to God. Stated so simply, I am sure almost every Christian would agree with this idea. Virtually all of us know the words, "Jesus loves me, this I know." As you can see in the opening line of this children's song, we are exposed to the concept of God's love almost as soon as we enter the doors of the church. Signs proclaiming the familiar John 3:16 are lifted in stadiums every weekend in this country. Tracts universally begin with, "God loves you." If there is one thing we want nonbelievers to know, it is "God loves you." Then why don't *we* know it?

This chapter presents another one of those difficult contradictions, statements made in isolation of each other that cannot both be true, but that we readily accept. We think this works for us, as long as we keep the two beliefs compartmentalized. However, compartmentalization creates internal division, which is unhealthy, as we have discussed. So, here are the two beliefs, overtly stated together: I matter to God (Jesus loves me), but I don't matter (it isn't about me). Can *you* make this make sense? I can't.

I believe that we as Christians are so fearful of being seen as arrogant or prideful that we adopt the opposite extreme of the same spectrum. We say, "I am worthless," and we feel very holy declaring it. Pride oozes from that self-debasing, self-righteous position, yet we don't see it. Somehow, we fool ourselves into thinking we are being humble. We call it righteous-sounding religious phrases, such as "dying to self," or "taking up our cross," having no notion of what either of those phrases really means. How did we arrive at this contradiction?

As we have already discussed, the church has conformed to culture instead of transforming it. Thus, American Christians seem to live out of many of our cultural beliefs in our spiritual lives. The attitude that elevates independence as the premier lifestyle is one such cultural value, as we have mentioned. Another is a hierarchical view of life, self, and others. It is as if we see ourselves as Mary Poppins, carrying around a bottomless bag, containing The Magic Ruler that assesses how we "measure up." The American ideal is success climbing the invisible ladder, whether that ladder is to get an A in school, to be the starter on the football team, to get the best job, to buy the biggest house, or to have the most money. The higher up the "ladder" we go, the better we "measure up." You can even see this hierarchical attitude reflected in the church: who has the tallest steeple in town, which church has the largest congregation, and which has the most money are frequent topics of conversation in church committee meetings.

Understand that I am not saying something is wrong with making A's in school, making the team, or having a successful business. I taught my own children to always be their best in all their endeavors, and I modeled the same principle for them while getting a Ph.D. and starting my own counseling practice. Being your best as equipped by God is a good, positive goal. The problem is not in the outcome; it is in the motivation. If I am making A's to elevate my status and secure my self-image as "good enough", these are the wrong motivations. If I am measuring my value based on the success of my business, this is the wrong gauge. Any external measure of my worth is potentially transient and temporary, easily threatened, undermined, or destroyed. Paul talks about his motivation for preaching the gospel:

> If I preach voluntarily, I have a reward; if not voluntarily, I am simply discharging the trust committed to me. What then is my reward? Just this: that in preaching the gospel I may offer it free of charge, and so not make use of my rights in preaching it. Though I am free and belong to no man, I make myself a slave to everyone, to win as many as possible...I do all this for the sake of the gospel, that I may share in its blessings. Do you not know that in a race all runners run, but only one gets the prize? Run in such a way as to get the prize. Everyone who competes in the games goes into strict training. They do it to get a crown that will not last; but we do it to get a crown that will last forever. Therefore I do not run like a man running aimlessly; I do not fight like a man beating the air. No, I beat my body and make it my slave so that after I have preached to others, I myself will not be disqualified for the prize. (I Corinthians 9:17-19, 25-27)

Divergent from our values, Paul is not talking about receiving "rewards" or "blessings" like a lot of money or a new car or big house. In fact, he makes the point earlier in this same letter that he is not accepting payment for his preaching; something he explains he has every right to do:

> If we have sown spiritual seed among you, is it too much if we reap a material harvest from you? If others have this right of support from you, shouldn't we have it all the more? But we did not use this right. On the contrary, we put up with anything rather than hinder the gospel of Christ. Don't you know that those who work in the

temple get their food from the temple, and those who serve at the altar share in what is offered on the altar? In the same way, the Lord has commanded that those who preach the gospel should receive their living from the gospel. But I have not used any of these rights. And I am not writing this in the hope that you will do such things for me. (1 Corinthians 9:11-15)

Paul is not talking about what he personally gets out of it. On the contrary, his reward is offering the gospel free of charge, and his motivation is to reach as many as possible. What are the "blessings" he refers to sharing in? Paul sees other believers as the blessings of the gospel. He is not seeking hierarchical position or esteem any more than he is seeking money or things. This conviction is obvious when, in I Corinthians 3, he confronts the Corinthian church with their identification as "followers of Paul," or someone else, other than Christ, and in verse 21 states, "So then, no more boasting about men!" In other words, Paul's self-image is not based on how many believers claim to be his followers, and the numbers making that claim does not measure his value to Christ. He goes on to say, "all things are yours…and you are of Christ, and Christ is of God (I Corinthians 3:22-23)." Is the absence of a hierarchy clear in these verses? Paul is describing all of God's children being on the same plane, with Christ. Paul knows he belongs to Christ and is God's child, and that is the essence of value. This lesson is the one Paul is conveying to the Corinthian church. He is telling them, in essence, they themselves are Christ's blessing, the crown that lasts forever, and God's "sacred temple" (I Corinthians 3:17).

You may be thinking that this description sounds very much like Paul is saying, "it is not about me." This is not the case, as I will explain. In the description of self-based lies referred to in an earlier chapter, we discussed pride and self-debasement as the two sides of the same "self coin." Examples of pride beliefs include "I am more important than," "I am better than," and "I am above it or others." This self-centered viewpoint negates others and elevates self, takes from others for selfish gain, and makes choices for the benefit of self at another's expense. The opposite side of the same coin would sound like, "I am worthless," "I am less or lower than," and, interestingly enough, "I don't matter." This equally self-centered perspective negates self and elevates others, allows others to use and abuse as if it is deserved, and reinforces its own belief by despising self. The main point of significance to understand about self-lies is they prevent the presence of love.

Paul is clear his preaching the gospel is not about his selfish gain, his personal elevation to a higher status, or any self-centered agenda. However, Paul is not in any way indicating that he does not matter. Quite the opposite. Paul is very clear that he matters to God, and he is stating clearly how much each individual also matters to God. There is no hierarchical measuring up. Every believer is on the same plane: beloved of God. As he instructs each Corinthian believer to "run in such a way as to get the prize," at the same time he is stating he does not "run like a man running aimlessly," but runs for the prize as well. The culmination of the understanding of our value, how much we matter, is seen in the nature of the prize, which is our relationship with God and relationships with as many others as can be brought to share in a relationship with God. Stated simply, the "prize" is shared love. I am reminded of the greatest commandments that summarize the whole Law, stated in both the Old Testament and the New Testament: love God with all your heart, and love your neighbor as yourself. In true love, there are no self-based lies (me taking from others for my gain, or me hating myself), but love *is* truly about me (freely given, freely received, freely returned). Who could stand at the foot of the cross, and seeing Christ hanging there for their sake, not feel loved? Who could witness such an act of complete love on their behalf and not know how much they mattered? The answer is, only someone consumed in the self-based lies of pride and self-denigration could arrive at the conclusion, "it is not about me," while seeing Jesus on the cross. Self-lies such as "I don't matter" actually impede our knowing the extent of God's love for us, rather than promote any kind of "humility." Self-lies stop us from receiving God's love freely, and therefore prevent us from fully loving God in response. All that is accomplished by self-debasement is that I end up on the bottom of the hierarchical ladder. May I point out, however, that I am still *on the ladder*. Any position on the ladder of pride (heads or tails) is the wrong plane to stand on, according to God's truth.

One problem with the hierarchical mind-set is that it is an up-and-down perspective. The invisible "ladder" is endless. In other words, there is always another rung. Ultimately, this hierarchical view means I can never be "good enough." Do you see the connection here between the described false belief of attempting to earn our salvation through works, and this false belief of "never being good enough?" Feeling we are not good enough, we try to climb the acceptability-to-God "ladder" and improve our position on it. However, someone will always be higher up than me, and someone will always be lower than me. The higher ones I envy, and the lower ones I judge, disdain, or criticize. Hopefully, you recognize these attitudes as not conforming to the likeness of Christ. If the fruit is bad, the root is bad. In this case, the root belief in hierarchy is the mistaken beginning point that leads to this type of ugly fruit.

In addition, hierarchy precludes partnership, and results instead in self-effort. Here is the fuel for pride. It is up to me to climb, and my success would be rendered irrelevant if I climbed successfully because I was in partnership with someone else. No, the rung I am on is mine alone, and I am reaching for the next one up in my own power and strength. Stepping on others to gain ground and leaving others behind is a matter of course. I expect to get stepped on and left behind as well, so I view others with varying levels of suspicion and mistrust. In any case, the burden is on my shoulders to reach the highest possible position, and I grope and struggle and strain with all my might to keep moving on up. Oh, I might give appropriate self-righteous lip service to "God's help," but I do not experience it within my heart. I view my ultimate position on the ladder as all up to me.

Finally, self-degradation comes when I "fall." Just as there is no top to the ladder, and no end going up, there is also no end to the downward drop. I can plummet into depression, and even contemplate suicide as a result of a slip. If who I am and my worth are measured by my position, I can lose myself at any moment...and I know it. On some deep, base level within me, I know the "I," defined by my place on the hierarchy, can disappear in an instant. As a result, I live in constant, unrelenting fear. Climbing the ladder becomes like a driven survival instinct. Anxiety is the predominant state of my being. On the other hand, perhaps I am one of those individuals who have tried to climb and found it too hard, or who have accepted without needing to try a conviction that I am incapable and unacceptable, so I have given up. Resignation and an adopted belief of futility determine my choice to stay on the "bottom rung." With a "what difference does it make" attitude, I pursue instead what I refer to as "fillers," those things in life such as

alcohol, drugs, pornography, gluttony, or unhealthy relationships that I think might fill up the emptiness I feel, and that I
use as replacements for the presence of God.

Paul taught against a hierarchical view. He wrote, "You are
all sons of God through faith in Christ Jesus, for all of you
who were baptized into Christ have clothed yourselves with
Christ. There is neither Jew nor Greek, slave nor free, male nor
female, for you are all one in Christ Jesus (Galatians 3:26-28)."
Restated, we are all on the same "plane," because we are one
with Christ, and therefore one with each other in Christ. Jesus
removes the hierarchies, the judgments, the scales, the Magic
Rulers, and the invisible ladders from our lives. I am not "better
than," nor am I "worse than." I am very simply His child.

Being His child defines me. By definition, therefore, I matter. Where does this truth leave me standing? My relationship
with God determines the new plane I am on instead of any
hierarchical position on the "ladder." On this new relational
plane, there is no room for judgment or condemnation, no view
of self over *or* under others, and no pride issues. I stand in freedom to respond out of genuine love because I have been loved,
starting with God first, and flowing through His relationship
with me into my heart. Then and only then is that genuine,
unadulterated love free to flow out into others. Security in my
relationship with Jesus gives me this ground on which to stand,
where I can serve freely instead of out of obligation. Just as
God is under no obligation to deem me "righteous" according
to my works, but freely offers righteousness as His gift, any
service I offer is given freely as a gift, or it is not real service. I
emphasize here that the gift begins with God's grace gift to me.
Without His gift, I have nothing genuine to offer, for my "giving"
would then come from a selfish motivation. The wrong motivation turns "giving" into taking. What I am describing here

is what Paul refers to as being conformed to the likeness of Christ, which *is God's purpose.*

Thus, there is no unseen Plan or unknown grand God-agenda. I am God's agenda! You are God's agenda! Each individual child of God is the complete and total focus of His Master Plan. His love for each one of us establishes and expresses this truth. What has been His Plan since the beginning? At creation, according to the Genesis story, His desire was to walk side by side with us, and to partner with us in everything. His Plan hasn't changed! The only thing that has evolved is the question of how He would accomplish the goal. First we were righteous, made in His image. Then, because of our sin, God credited our faith as righteousness. The Law was given to identify sin for us, and to make clear our need for His gift of grace, for we forgot we even had a Partner. Finally, He loved us unto death, even death on the cross, reestablishing our faith as righteousness through His love and merciful gift. Always, the Plan was and is to have relationship with us, to love us, to create oneness with us, and to partner with us. Solely through His actions on our behalf, our hearts are transformed back to the original state of His creation, and we are able to love Him with all our hearts. The Plan is completed with the flow of His love from our hearts toward others in genuine service, again not by our effort or ability, but simply by His presence living in our hearts. Rather than diminishing God's majesty, glory and wonder, I am left in jaw-dropping awe at the lengths He goes to on my behalf, and the unbounded nature of His love for me.

Chapter 12

Conclusion

Bringing it All Together

THERE ARE MANY WONDERFUL ONE-LINERS FROM THE STAR
Trek movies and series. One of my favorites, spoken by Scotty
in *Star Trek III: The Search for Spock*, seems a relevant beginning for this concluding chapter (to be read in brogue): "The
more they over-think the plumbing, the easier it is to clog up
the drain."

In my experiences, Jesus' teachings in my heart have been
simple truths; not simplistic, not simple-minded, but profound
in their simplicity. Take, for example, the image of me standing
on the bottom of the ocean with no chance of making it to the
surface. The simple truth? Without Jesus, I am dead already.
While a straightforward and basic statement, this truth is also
a weighty realization, and deeply meaningful.

I contrast this profound simplicity with the complicated,
convoluted compartmentalization in current church dogma,
or the one-dimensional, step-wise, fill-in-the-blank nature of
many sermons and Christian books, and I just don't see the
presence of the Spirit of Christ. I am left with the feeling that

the church's plumbing is clogged. Has our self-reliance caused us to "over-think" the gospel? Have the simple truths of Christ escaped us, to be replaced by lists of clever-sounding but meaningless phrases and complex theological premises attempting to replace the Holy Spirit leading us into all truth? Instead of a relationship, has our faith become a banking transaction? Having lost what we once knew, are we trying to recreate it without the leading of its Creator?

Refer back now to the opening sentence of the opening chapter. In a sense, Scotty's statement is really describing the process of entropy, the tendency toward chaos and disorder. Humans, just as molecules in the physical realm, tend to expend increasing amounts of energy to move toward greater and higher levels of confusion. We make what is simple complicated. We take what is clear and muddy the waters. We transform basic truths into ever-growing thought structures built upon layers of thin air, and we believe the complexity of our "building" gives it meaning and makes it profound. However, what we create is not deep and meaningful, but empty. Our beliefs have become shallow and hollow.

Over the years, I have been asked many times by many people to write a book. Up to this point, I have refused, saying it would be the shortest book in history consisting of only two words: Ask Jesus. My understanding of the laws of physics and the nature of entropy helped me to see the need to input energy into the "system" of the church in order to combat the tendency toward chaos. So, instead of two words, we end up with twelve chapters. Nevertheless, the ideas in this book are actually quite simple. Most of the energy of this writing has been to undo the current state of belief. Now, we will bring it back to the simple truths of who God is, and who He says we are.

Tying Together Historical Perspectives

Since Paul represents for us the earliest example of a Christian theology that was taught to multiple groups of people in different regions, we have examined many aspects of his letters in these chapters, and come to some (hopefully) interesting conclusions about his beliefs. We have seen that Paul's gospel was not stories about the life and teachings of Jesus, but instead began with Jesus' death. We have discussed how Paul firmly believed that Jesus was the fulfillment of God's promise to Abraham, and that the God of Abraham and the God of Jesus were perceived to be the same figure. We have discussed mystery in the Greek context of revelation of knowledge, rather than an unknowable secret. We have explored the Hellenized Jewish world and the value Paul placed on logical thought. We have analyzed Paul's conceptual matrix of faith. We have discussed Paul's beliefs about suffering and the modern misperceptions about the Roman Empire during the time of Jesus and the first Christians. We have explained Paul's apocalyptic beliefs, his perceptions of a spiritual war, and his conviction that God would recapture authority over the world from Satan and his followers. We have made the distinction between Paul's beliefs in independence (as material self-sufficiency) and freedom (as spiritual slavery to God). We have enumerated the roles that the Spirit of God played in Paul's theology. We have clarified Paul's position on works, as opposed to his conception of faith. We have discussed how Paul placed behavior as secondary to and coming out of love and "freedom" given by dependence on God. Finally, we have explained that Paul believed humanity to be of great worth to God, and that God's purpose is to conform those who love Him to the likeness of Jesus.

It is now my task to gather the many different beliefs we have discussed throughout this book and to present Paul's theology in one place. Paul's beliefs began with his Jewish context. Raised an upright Jew, Paul originally persecuted the earliest followers of Jesus. Having experienced a profound event in which he believed he met Jesus firsthand, Paul's life completely changed. He began preaching the same message of the people he once persecuted. The gospel that Paul preached to his churches was one of simplicity: Jesus died as payment for the sins of mankind, God raised him, and he would return at the end to judge mankind. However, he did not abandon his Jewish context. Instead, he believed Jesus was the ultimate fulfillment of God's promise to Abraham. This death and resurrection made it possible again for mankind to be justified by faith (as Abraham had once been). Faith began by first hearing this message (as Abraham had heard God and Paul believed he had heard Jesus). Then, the hearer would be convinced of the trustworthiness of God (as Abraham had believed God and as Paul was convinced by his encounter).

This conviction (through hearing the gospel) would result in calling out and surrender to God. Surrender obtains access to the gift of grace (given through the death and resurrection of Jesus), freedom from sin (as slavery to God), the elevation of the person to the status of child of God and heir to God's kingdom, and the gift of God's Spirit. Since Paul believed there was a supernatural war waging, God's Spirit gives the person the weapons of spiritual warfare (to demolish arguments and deceit), allowing others to be convinced (by hearing the gospel) and surrender to God (and receive the same grace and Spirit). Also as a result of the Spirit of God (not because of any "works"), the person begins fulfilling God's purpose (being conformed to the likeness of Jesus). This conforming process begins in the heart and results in changed behaviors. The behaviors produced come from the knowledge of the love of

God (manifested through Jesus' death and resurrection and the gift of grace), and the confidence in the person's position as Jesus' sibling, God's child, and co-heir to the kingdom (all of which came from slavery to God). Thus, out of love and certainty of freedom, the person will willingly give up his or her position (as Jesus gave up his position of "equality to God" and Paul gave up his "permissible" freedoms), and will become a servant (as Jesus "made himself nothing, taking on the very nature of a servant" and Paul became "all things to all people"). These behaviors are representative of the process of fulfilling God's purpose, which is each individual being conformed to the likeness of Jesus.

Tying It All Together Toward Restoration

Everything begins with God's deep and adoring love for each and every one of us. I almost hate to write this sentence, because it sounds like so much traditional fluff without any personal meaning. However, to achieve the restoration we desire, we *must get past* the empty, trite and superficial perceptions resulting from overuse and misuse, and *redefine* our language. I am not speaking about some generic love. He knows His children intimately and individually, uniquely and personally. Nor I am talking about a cheap and easy love. I do not toss the term around lightly, like we often do about loving our new outfit, loving our new car, or even loving our spouse. His love is not bestowed from a distance. He is not "up there" or "out there." He is not a bad daddy, inconsistent and unpredictable, absent or punishing, capricious or abusive. It is not love devoid of action, for the choice has been made and the expression of love fulfilled on the cross. There is no selfishness in this love, unlike the kind we profess as love that is actually very self-gratifying.

This love is the look in the eyes of the King as he breathes deeply his rapturous passion for Anna. This love is the gentleness of the hand that shares His air with the drowning diver before she ever realizes she needs it, and it is the strength of the Rescuer hauling that diver to the surface, carrying her full weight all the way. This love is the patience of the One sitting beside the sailor in the boat, waiting through the terrible storm for her to finally see Him there so He can take her safely to shore. This love is the fierce and protective determination of Sam as he lifts Frodo onto his shoulders to fight the final fight, so Frodo could be done with the burden of evil once and for all.

These are my "visions" of the love Jesus has for me. I believe each individual child of God can have his or her own image or way of knowing that love. I also believe each relationship with Jesus is unique, a "wedding" of two becoming one that is defined by the natures of the two partners. A personal way of saying this is that Jesus sees and knows me, Helga Anna, intimately in every detail, and He loves me *for who I am*. Another person, with another name and another identity, He would also love, but for who that individual is, not for anything resembling what He knows and loves about Helga Anna. In addition, each special relationship produces its own unique fruit. I have described this with the statement, "If there had been no Handel, there would be no Handel's Messiah." Only Handel, with God's partnership, would have produced that specific result. Does this give you any insight at all into how much we matter to God? It is quite amazing that God chose to make us His partners in creation, letting us have a hand in what is produced, whether it is the beauty of music or the ugliness of the consequences of sin.

For me, these "visions" of God's love I have described are word-pictures of something that I *know* in the very core of my being, in the depths of my heart, in every cell in my body. Even if Billy Graham and Mother Theresa both walked up to me and told me Jesus loved or saw me differently from what I know is true, or that His nature was other than the One I know, I would simply shake my head sadly and say, "I'm sorry you feel that way." This is not arrogance on my part; it is the certainty of knowing. This unwavering certainty is the conviction that is faith, as Paul describes it. Faith is not wishful thinking; it is knowledge. Having heard the truth from the Spirit, I am absolutely and firmly convinced of it. I believe that it is that very certainty, knowing God instead of settling for knowing about God, that the church has lost.

We don't speak boldly for we are not sure enough to do so. We rely on such explanations as "we can never fully understand the mysteries of God" to cover up our own insecurity. We explain away things in our experiences that don't match our beliefs with an admonition that we "just have to have faith." Rather than seeking the truth from the Holy Spirit, as Paul taught early followers to do, we compartmentalize our beliefs into independent and contradictory subcategories, and try to assimilate God into our own understanding. We resort to fear tactics to try and muscle people into belief, foregoing the power of the Holy Spirit's weapons to dissimilate deceptions and persuade others of the truth, because we don't know or trust that He will do so. We separate Jesus from our daily lives into a spiritual-only involvement, and then take the rest of our lives into our own hands. And when things fall apart or we face suffering, we "credit" God for the difficulties as lessons to be learned or refining we need to get better at doing His stuff, toward our small "purpose" in His Master Plan.

If we were to give all these things up for the opportunity to know Jesus in the core of our beings, in the very deepest parts of our hearts, where would that leave us? Personally, I think we are afraid of the answer to that question and that is why we do not ask. It is an unknown, and unfamiliar to us. Still, I believe surrender into a relationship-centered view takes us to a new and better place. Instead of undermining our faith, seeking to know only Jesus strengthens our knowledge and our certainty.

So, I begin with God's love for me. From that position, I begin to cultivate that trust that every relationship requires before it can have intimacy. Trust comes from knowing Who God is, and knowing what to expect from Him. That means I must be willing to give up all of my preconceptions, and approach Him "as a child," willing to see Him anew and asking Him to remove anything that is in my way. Sometimes, my experiences in this world are in the way, as they may have taught me beliefs that are false about myself, about life, and about God. I do not ask God to change my experiences, for this would not be reality, but I ask Him to change my beliefs about those experiences. Simply put, I ask Him to identify whatever perceptions are false and to replace them with the truth. Using my earlier analogy of being told the sky is green my whole life, I ask Him to take me outside and show me the sky. Bad theology is another possibility of what can get in the way of our understanding God. It is our hope that this book has been a starting point for making those theological changes, and that God will plow the ground in those who can receive the seeds offered here, so that they can take root and grow.

As the process of seeing and knowing Jesus unfolds, I can also ask Him to show me who I am. My own experience with Jesus taught me that I could not fully know the answer to that question until I knew Who God was, but I want to leave room for unique personal experiences. Your relationship development progression may look very different from what I describe from my own process. For me, asking Him to give me my new name (as He gave to Abraham, Peter, and Paul) was my starting point in seeing who He created me to be. I encourage you to allow Him to lead you into that knowledge in whatever way only He knows is the best road to take for your sake.

This seems a good time to reiterate that I am not attempting to create a "list" of steps to follow. If you can't tell by this point in the book that I despise "lists of six", as I call them, you probably need to go back and reread earlier chapters! My goal from the beginning has been to describe in general terms what elements are present in a deep and intimate relationship with God. I am relying completely on the Holy Spirit to accomplish whatever needs to happen in your heart for your own relationship with Him to come to fruition. I likened this process to marital counseling, where I cannot know the individual preferences or desires of your spouse in relation to you, but I can describe to you generally what works in a marriage and what does not. For example, I am a very visual learner. Therefore, Jesus teaches me in pictures, for in my mind and heart, a picture expresses a lot more than words ever could. I am very aware, though, that some people are auditory learners and some are more tactile or experiential. Each individual's relationship with Jesus will be reflective of that individual's unique nature. He knows what works best with you, and He will use it to its fullest to reach you. Don't be bound up in trying to follow an arbitrary set of "steps," but walk hand-in-hand with Jesus to find your own path.

I believe that knowing Who God is and knowing who He says I am are the "root truths" I need, and that all other truths grow from those roots. Where I go from there is into the type of relationship that deep love and trust creates. It is a relationship where I prefer to be with Him above anyone else. The relationship includes a level of communication where I share honestly, openly, and completely each and every moment, thought, and feeling, no matter what the context. I can talk to Him about anything, and I choose to talk to Him about everything. He is there for me in every experience, from the everyday to the exceptional to the excruciating, as my partner, my support, and my love. He shows me the best choices for my benefit, and the best paths to take. He holds me and cries with me and comforts me when I need it. He guides me in decisions, but never decides for me. His arms are strong, His shoulders are soft, and His eyes convey love beyond my ability to express in words. All I can say is an encouragement that He wants to share these things with you, and that you can know Him, too.

As we conclude, we turn back to Cody, who stands in our lives as an example of what an intimate relationship with Jesus can be like, and the fruit it produces. He might have every reason to be discouraged or bitter or fearful, but he is not. Instead, he has an ease in his life, a peace and a joy that healthy people, who have no apparent reason for anything else but ease, most often do not have. What does he know that others don't? What does he have that others are missing? He would say, quite simply, he shares everything, each breath he takes, with Jesus. This is a significant statement, because breathing appears to us to be so problematic for him. He would say it is not. He would say, and always does say, that he is "fine." Someone watching him would not think he was "fine," and I suppose you might think the observer knows better. We would say Cody knows the truth. His circumstances have no power over him. He knows only Christ, and that is all he needs to know.

May we all find that place.

Notes

[1] I I will attempt to keep notes to a minimum, in order to avoid detracting from the flow of the chapters. All quotations from the Bible come from the New International Version, unless otherwise noted.

[2] Barna, George. *Growing True Disciples: New Strategies for Producing Genuine Followers of Christ*. Colorado Springs, CO: WaterBrook Press, 2001.

[3] Frend, W.H.C. *The Early Church*. Minneapolis, MN: Fortress Press, 1982; Sanders, E.P. *The Historical Figure of Jesus*. London: Penguin Books, 1993; ibid. *Jesus and Judaism*. Philadelphia: Fortress, 1985.

[4] Ehrman, Bart. *The New Testament: A Historical Introduction to the Early Christian Writings*, 3rd Ed. New York: Oxford University Press, 2004; ibid. *Peter, Paul, and Mary Magdalene: The Followers of Jesus in History and Legend*. New York: Oxford University Press, 2006.

[5] Ehrman, *The New Testament: A Historical Introduction to the Early Christian Writings*; Bibles that contain historical information usually record these historical dates as well.

[6] For a more detailed study on methods of examining the Gospel stories, see Ehrman, *The New Testament: A Historical Introduction to the Early Christian Writings*; see also Sanders, *The Historical Figure of Jesus*.

[7] Eisenstein, Elizabeth L. *The Printing Revolution in Early Modern Europe*. Cambridge: Cambridge University Press, 1983, 2005.

[8] Jaroslav Pelikan addresses the changes in the interpretation of Jesus in Christian theologies through time; *Jesus through the Centuries.* New Haven, Connecticut: Yale University Press, 1985.

[9] Craig L. Blomberg has a similar list of Paul's quotations, though he attributes to Jesus any statement that Paul makes which is in any way similar to something from the four Gospels; "Where do we Start Studying Jesus?" In *Jesus Under Fire.* Zondervan, 1995, pp.41.

[10] Ehrman, *The New Testament: A Historical Introduction to the Early Christian Writings.*

[11] Ibid.

[12] Frend, W.H.C. *The Early Church.* Minneapolis, MN: Fortress Press, 1982; Metzger, Bruce M. *The Canon of the New Testament.* New York: Oxford University Press, 1987; White, L. Michael. *From Jesus to Christianity.* San Francisco: HarperCollins, 2004.

[13] Sanders, E.P. *Paul and Palestinian Judaism.* Augsburg Fortress Publishers, 1977; Ehrman, *Peter, Paul, and Mary Magdalene: The Followers of Jesus in History and Legend.*

[14] Kottak, Conrad Phillip. *Cultural Anthropology,* 9th Ed. New York: McGraw Hill, 2001.

[15] Burkert, Walter. *Ancient Mystery Cults.* Cambridge: Harvard University Press, 1987.

[16] Momigliano, Arnaldo. *On Pagans, Jews, and Christians.* Middletown, Connecticut: Wesleyan University Press, 1987; Lloyd, G. E. R. *Magic, Reason and Experience: Studies in the Origins and Development of Greek Science.* Indianapolis: Hackett Publishing Company, Inc., 1979, 1999.

[17] Cederblom, Jerry and David Paulson. *Critical Reasoning,* 6th Ed. New York: Wadsworth Publishing, 2005.

[18] For a discussion of *pistis* in the context of evidentiary grounds for faith, see David M. Hay, "Pistis as 'Ground for Faith' in Hellenized Judaism and Paul." *JBL* 108 (1989) pp. 461-476.

[19] Ehrman, Bart. *The New Testament: A Historical Introduction to the Early Christian Writings,* 3rd Ed. New York: Oxford University Press, 2004; Sanders, E.P. *The Historical Figure of Jesus.* London: Penguin Books, 1993.

[20] Armstrong, *A History of God;* Frend, *The Early Church.*

[21]Ehrman, *The New Testament: A Historical Introduction to the Early Christian Writings*; Nock, A. D. *Conversion: The Old and the New in Religion from Alexander the Great to Augustine of Hippo.* Baltimore, MD: The Johns Hopkins University Press, 1933; Sanders, *The Historical Figure of Jesus*; Smith, Morton. *Jesus the Magician: Charlatan or Son of God?* Berkeley, California: Seastone, 1978, 1998.

[22]Ehrman, *The New Testament: A Historical Introduction to the Early Christian Writings.*

[23]According to a nationwide survey conducted by the Barna Research Institute, 82% of Americans believe this phrase comes directly from the Bible; George Barna "What Effective Churches Have Learned" Seminar at Capital Christian Center, 1996.

[24]Pelikan, *Jesus through the Centuries.*

[25]Veyne, Paul. *Did the Greeks Believe in their Myths?* Trans. Paula Wissing. University of Chicago Press, 1988; François de Polignac. *Cults, Territory, and the Origins of the Greek City-State.* Trans. Janet Lloyd. University of Chicago Press, 1995.

[26]"It isn't about you" is the very first statement found in *The Purpose Driven Life*; Rick Warren, Grand Rapids, MI: Zondervan, 2002; see also Max Lucado, *It's Not About Me.* Nashville: Integrity Publishers, 2004.

Bibliography

Modern Authors

Andrews, Elias. *The Meaning of Christ for Paul*. Nashville: Abington-Cokesbury Press, 1949.

Armstrong, Karen. *A History of God*. New York: Ballantine Books, 1993.

Barna, George. *Growing True Disciples: New Strategies for Producing Genuine Followers of Christ*. Colorado Springs, CO: WaterBrook Press, 2001.

Barnstone, Willis, ed. *The Other Bible: Ancient Alternative Scriptures*. New York: HarperCollins, 1984.

Blackaby, Henry. *Experiencing God*. Nashville: Broadman & Holman, 1994.

Blomberg, Craig L. *The Historical Reliability of the Gospels*. Downers Grove, Illinois: InterVarsity Press, 1987.

Brother Lawrence, *The Practice of the Presence of God*. In *Practicing his Presence: The Library of Spiritual Classics*, Vol. I. Jacksonville, FL: The SeedSowers, 1973

Burkert, Walter. *Ancient Mystery Cults*. Cambridge: Harvard University Press, 1987.

Cederblom, Jerry and David Paulson. *Critical Reasoning*, 6th Ed. New York: Wadsworth Publishing, 2005.

Crossan, John Dominic and Jonathan L. Reed. *Excavating Jesus*. San Francisco: HarperCollins, 2001.

Curtis, Brent and Eldredge, John. *The Sacred Romance*. Nashville: Thomas Nelson Inc., 1997.

de Polignac, François. *Cults, Territory, and the Origins of the Greek City-State*. Trans. Janet Lloyd. Chicago: University of Chicago Press, 1995.

Dobson, James. *When God Doesn't Make Sense*. Wheaton, Illinois: Tyndale House, 1983.

Ehrman, Bart. *Lost Scriptures*. New York: Oxford University Press, 2003.

Ehrman, Bart. *Misquoting Jesus*. New York: HarperCollins, 2005.

Ehrman, Bart. *The New Testament: A Historical Introduction to the Early Christian Writings*, 3rd Ed. New York: Oxford University Press, 2004.

Ehrman, Bart. *Peter, Paul, and Mary Magdalene: The Followers of Jesus in History and Legend*. New York: Oxford University Press, 2006.

Eisenstein, Elizabeth L. *The Printing Revolution in Early Modern Europe*. Cambridge: Cambridge University Press, 1983, 2005

Eldredge, John. *The Journey of Desire*. Nashville: Thomas Nelson Inc., 2000.

Evans, Craig A. *Fabricating Jesus: How Modern Scholars Distort the Gospel*. Downers Grove, Illinois: InterVarsity Press, 2006.

Foster, Richard. *Celebration of Discipline*. San Francisco: HarperSanFrancisco, 1978.

Foster, Richard. *Streams of Living Water*. San Francisco: HarperSanFrancisco, 2001.

Frend, W.H.C. *The Early Church*. Minneapolis, MN: Fortress Press, 1982.

Funk, Robert W., Roy W. Hoover and the Jesus Seminar. *The Five Gospels: What Did Jesus Really Say?* New York: Macmillan, 1993.

Harnack, Adolf. *What is Christianity?* New York: Harper Torchbooks, 1902, 1957.

Hay, David M. "Pistis as 'Ground for Faith' in Hellenized Judaism and Paul." *JBL* 108 (1989) pp. 461-476.

Hudson, Joyce Rockwood. *Natural Spirituality: Recovering the Wisdom Tradition in Christianity*. Danielsville, GA: JRH Publications, 2000.

Kasser, Rodolphe, Marvin Meyer, and Gregor Wurst, eds. "The Gospel of Judas." *The National Geographic Society*, 2006.

Kottak, Conrad Phillip. *Cultural Anthropology*, 9th Ed. New York: McGraw Hill, 2001.

Lewis, C. S. *Mere Christianity*. San Francisco: HarperSanFrancisco, 1952.

Lloyd, G. E. R. *Magic, Reason and Experience: Studies in the Origins and Development of Greek Science*. Indianapolis: Hackett Publishing Company, Inc., 1979, 1999.

Lotz, Anne Graham. *My Heart's Cry*. Nashville: W Publishing Group, 2002.

Lucado, Max. *It's Not About Me*. Nashville: Integrity Publishers, 2004.

MacArthur, John. *The Truth War*. Nashville: Thomas Nelson, Inc. 2007.

Markus, R. A. *The End of Ancient Christianity*. Cambridge: Cambridge University Press, 1990.

Metzger, Bruce M. *The Canon of the New Testament*. New York: Oxford University Press, 1987.

Momigliano, Arnaldo. *On Pagans, Jews, and Christians*. Middletown, Connecticut: Wesleyan University Press, 1987.

Moore, Beth. *Breaking Free*. B&H Publishers, 2000.

Nock, A. D. *Conversion: The Old and the New in Religion from Alexander the Great to Augustine of Hippo*. Baltimore, MD: The Johns Hopkins University Press, 1933.

Nouwen, Henri J. M. *Reaching Out: The Three Movements of the Spiritual Life*. New York: Doubleday, 1975.

Ogden, Greg. *Transforming Discipleship: Making Disciples a Few at a Time*. Downer's Grove, IL: InterVarsity Press, 2003.

Omartian, Stormie. *The Power of a Praying Wife*. Eugene, Oregon: Harvest House Publishers, 1997.

Pelikan, Jaroslav. *Jesus through the Centuries*. New Haven, Connecticut: Yale University Press, 1985.

Piper, John. *Desiring God*. Colorado Springs, Colorado: Multnomah Publishers, 1986.

Piper, John. *What Jesus Demands From the World*. Wheaton, Illinois: Crossway Books, 2006.

Sanders, E.P. *The Historical Figure of Jesus*. London: Penguin Books, 1993.

Sanders, E.P. *Jesus and Judaism*. Philadelphia: Fortress, 1985.

Sanders, E.P. *Paul and Palestinian Judaism*. Augsburg Fortress Publishers, 1977.

Sailhamer, John H. *Biblical Archaeology*. Grand Rapids, MI: Zondervan, 1998.

Seamands, David. *Healing for Damaged Emotions*. Victor Books, 1991.

Smith, Morton. *Jesus the Magician: Charlatan or Son of God?* Berkeley, California Seastone, 1978, 1998.

Soanes, Catherine and Angus Stevenson. *Concise Oxford English Dictionary*, 11th Ed. New York: Oxford University Press, 2004.

Spong, John Shelby. *A New Christianity for a New World*. New York: HarperCollins Publishers, Inc. 2001.

Spong, John Shelby. *Why Christianity Must Change or Die*. New York: HarperCollins Publishers, Inc. 1998.

Strobel, Lee. *The Case for Christ: A Journalist's Personal Investigation of the Evidence for Jesus*. Grand Rapids, MI: Zondervan, 1998.

Veyne, Paul. *Did the Greeks Believe in their Myths?* Trans. Paula Wissing. Chicago: University of Chicago Press, 1988.

Warren, Rick. *The Purpose Driven Life*. Grand Rapids, MI: Zondervan, 2002.

White, L. Michael. *From Jesus to Christianity*. San Francisco: HarperCollins, 2004.

Wilkins, Michael J and J.P. Moreland, eds. *Jesus Under Fire: Modern Scholarship Reinvents the Historical Jesus*. Grand Rapids, MI: Zondervan, 1995.

Wilkinson, Bruce. *The Prayer of Jabez*. Colorado Springs, Colorado: Multnomah Publishers, 2000.

Yancy, Philip. *Jesus I Never Knew*. Grand Rapids, Michigan: Zondervan, 1995.

Yancy, Philip. *What's So Amazing About Grace?* Grand Rapids, Michigan: Zondervan, 1989.

Yancy, Philip. *Reaching for the Invisible God*. Grand Rapids, Michigan: Zondervan, 2000.

Yancy, Philip. *Where is God When It Hurts?* Grand Rapids, Michigan: Zondervan, 1990.

Ancient Authors

Athanasius, "Festal Letter XXXIX"

Eusebius, *Ecclesiastical History*

Irenaeus, *Against Heresies*

Josephus, *Jewish Antiquities*

   Against Apion

   Jewish War

Justin Martyr, *Apologia*

Lucian, *Alexander the False Prophet*

   The Death of Peregrinus

Philo of Alexandria, *Every Good Man is Free*

   Hypothetica

   Who is the Heir of Divine Things

   Special Laws

Plato, *Timaeus*

   Republic

Pliny, *Epistles*. Book X

Plutarch, *Parallel Lives*

Suetonius, *The Lives of the Twelve Caesars*: "The Deified Claudius"

Tacitus, *Annals*

Bibles

Archaeological Study Bible. NIV. Grand Rapids, Michigan: Zondervan, 2005.

Holy Bible, Catholic Edition. RSV. Camden, NJ: Thomas Nelson Publishers, 1966.

The Interlinear NASB-NIV Parallel New Testament in Greek and English. Trans. Alfred Marshall. Grand Rapids, Michigan: Zondervan, 1993.

PC Study Bible, Version 4.0

Other Media

A Charlie Brown Christmas. CBS, 1965.

Barna, George. "What Effective Churches Have Learned" Seminar at Capital Christian Center, 1996

Berlin, Irving. "Blue Skies," 1926.

Bruce Almighty. Universal Studios, 2003.

Dorsey, Tommy. "Santa Claus is Coming to Town," 1935.

"How it Works." *Rosetta Stone* website. Online, 2007. http://www.rosettastone.com/en/individuals/method

Snow White and the Seven Dwarves. Walt Disney Pictures, 1937.

Star Trek III: The Search for Spock. Paramount, 1984.

"The Best of Both Worlds: Parts I and II." *Star Trek: The Next Generation*. Paramount, 1990.

The Lord of the Rings: The Return of the King. New Line Cinema, 2003.

"The World is Hollow and I Have Touched the Sky." *Star Trek*. Paramount, 1968.

Printed in the United States
128213LV00001B/1/A